Rainbow Edition

Reading Mastery V
Skillbook

Siegfried Engelmann • Jean Osborn • Steve Osborn • Leslie Zoref

Macmillan/McGraw–Hill
Columbus, Ohio

SRA Macmillan/McGraw-Hill
250 Old Wilson Bridge Road
Suite 310
Worthington, Ohio 43085
Printed in the United States of America.
ISBN 0-02-686407-X
        5 6 7 8 9 0 COU 99 98 97

Lesson 3

PART A   Word Lists

1
cupboard
sober
celebration
Mombo

2
pineapple
haircut
airport
grassland
hideout

3
wood
wooden
terrible
terribly

4
Vocabulary words
1. peg
2. eager
3. inquire
4. glisten
5. mile
6. emeralds
7. diamonds

5
Vocabulary words
1. cupboard
2. sober
3. celebration
4. budge
5. bounding

6
loudly
perfectly
slowly
politely
suddenly
anxiously

PART B
Vocabulary Sentences

1. This room contained a rusty-looking stove and a <u>cupboard</u> for the dishes.
   ● cup   ● ceiling   ● cabinet
2. The sun and wind had taken the sparkle from her eyes and left them a <u>sober</u> gray.
   ● serious   ● happy   ● red
3. They had a great <u>celebration</u>.
   ● school   ● party   ● sleep
4. He tried to pull the post out of the ground, but the post would not <u>budge</u>.
   ● glisten   ● disappear   ● move
5. The animals were <u>bounding</u> swiftly down the tunnel.
   ● sitting   ● running   ● walking

PART C   Word Endings

● **Complete each item by adding the correct ending to the underlined word.**
1. The picture was <u>perfect</u>.
   It was painted _____ .
2. When he was hungry he would get <u>anxious</u>.
   So he waited for dinner _____ .
3. The young man was <u>polite</u>.
   So he acted _____ .
4. She had a <u>loud</u> voice.
   So she talked _____ .
5. The noise was <u>sudden</u>.
   So we heard it _____ .
6. The car was very <u>slow</u>.
   So it went very _____ .

PART D   Story Items

7. Where was Mr. Williams?
8. Who was unhappy because Mr. Williams was not in the house?

9. Jill left something that would let Mr. Williams know where Tom and Jill had gone.
   a. What did she leave?
   b. How far was it from their house to the tree with the hollow trunk?
   c. In which direction was the tree from the house?
10. a. When Jill and Tom arrived at the tree, who was sitting in the shade?
    b. Who was the first to go back inside the hollow tree?
    c. What did that person see inside the tree?
    d. Jill asked, "Do you speak English?" Who responded to that question?
    e. Who started to talk fast and make up stories?
    f. What was the name of the man?
    g. How often did the people from the village use the cave?

11. As Jill and the others talked, something happened that made the man think that there was something strange inside the cave. What happened?

12. **Write the correct word on your paper.**
Mombo told the others that the cave had ＿＿＿＿＿ of tunnels and rooms.

13. Mombo and the others followed Roger to the large room.
How did Mombo figure out which tunnel to follow on the other side of the room?

PART E   Review Items

14. **Use the words in the box to fill in the blanks or replace the underlined words.**

wonderful	cell	plain
poachers	howl	prepared
	serve	

a. There were fewer birds in the flock each year because ＿＿＿＿＿ kept taking them.

b. There was nothing but grass on the flat place with few trees.

c. They got ready for the horse ride by putting the saddle on.

d. Even though it rained, she had a marvelous time.

Lesson 4

PART A   Word Lists

1
sound
shout
bound
loudly
found

2
liver
deliver
terribly
wooden

3
Vocabulary words
1. CB radio
2. flutter
3. snarling
4. lanterns
5. peg
6. party
7. sober
8. bounding
9. celebration
10. budge

4
stiffly
thoughtfully
gratefully
quietly

PART B   Word Endings

● **Complete each item by adding the correct ending to the underlined word.**

1. She felt stiff.
So she walked ＿＿＿＿＿.

2. The little boy was thoughtful.
So he behaved ＿＿＿＿＿.

3. They were grateful.
So they thanked him ＿＿＿＿＿.

4. Deer are very quiet.
So the deer ran through the woods ＿＿＿＿＿.

PART C Story Items

5. a. Who was leading the way through the cave?
   b. How did he know which tunnel to follow from the large room?
   c. As the tunnel went down steeply, Tom said, "I can _____ something."
   d. Jill heard men's voices. Why were the men shouting?

6. **Write the correct choice on your paper.**
   a. What did one voice say to do?
      ● "Catch him!" ● "Grab him!"
      ● "Shoot him!"
   b. The room they came to was as big as a
      ● city   ● circus tent
      ● football field

7. a. Where did the light in the room come from?
   b. What did Jill notice on the far side of the room?
   c. She thought it led to the _____.

8. All around the rock walls of the cave were _____.

9. Jill and the others snuck into the large room. The men inside were talking about getting rid of somebody.
   a. Who?
   b. The animals that the poachers had were worth close to _____.

10. Something frightened Tom and made him shout.
    a. What frightened him?
    b. What did Mombo do as the men approached?

11. How much time did the poachers need to move the animals from the cave?
12. The poachers planned to keep _____ and _____ in a cage.
13. What was holding Jill's cage shut?
14. What was holding the doors to the animal cages closed?
    ● Large wooden pegs
    ● Poles   ● Large locks
15. What did Jill want to do if she got out of her cage?

PART D Review Items

16. **Use the words in the box to fill in the blanks or replace the underlined words.**

candle	emeralds	glistened
diamonds	haircut	inquired
brook	miles	

a. Robin's green dress was the same color as her _____.
b. When the clear water from the fountain shot up it looked like _____.
c. Charlotte ran for three _____.
d. When the cat's fur was wet it _____.
c. She <u>asked</u> about the distance to the store.

Lesson 5

PART A   Word Lists

1	2	3	4
cyclone	cackle	whirl	sure
prairie	candle	whirlwinds	pressure
Dorothy	tunnel	electric	fun
Aunt	sparkle	surround	funnel
Toto	incredible	surroundings	anxious
horizon	startle	orphan	usual
	twinkle	rough	anxiously
		deliver	

5
Vocabulary words
1. in spite of
2. attic
3. rust
4. horizon
5. snarling
6. lanterns

6
Vocabulary words
1. merrily
2. mass
3. cradle
4. wail
5. sober

PART B
Vocabulary Sentences

1. The dog was happy and his eyes twinkled <u>merrily</u>.
   - sadly   ● happily   ● meanly
2. The sun had baked the plowed land into a gray <u>mass</u>.
   - house   ● ice floe
   - area with no shape
3. She felt as if she was being rocked gently, like a baby in a <u>cradle</u>.
   - truck   ● small bed   ● pillow
4. From the far north, they heard a low <u>wail</u> of the wind.
   - sea animal   ● howl   ● squeak
5. His expression was not <u>sober</u>.
   - eager   ● happy   ● serious

PART C   Story Items

1. At the beginning of Part 5, Jill and Tom were in a cage.
   a. How many poachers were in the room?
   b. What did the poachers do after a while?
2. Who snuck into the room?
3. Jill called Roger from one side of the cage door to the other.
   a. Why did she do that?
   b. Did the plan work?
   c. Who stayed inside the cage?
4. Jill and Tom went to the other cages.
   a. What did they do to most of those cages?
   b. What wild animals did they leave in cages?
   c. When they were at one of the last cages, who made the animals start making noises?
   d. Which animal opened one of the cages?
5. Al started toward Jill. Who came into the room just then?
6. Who had called for three other rangers?

7. The next morning, Jill and Tom watched the rangers as they released the _____.
8. Mr. Williams announced that he was going to take a new job in _____.
9. How did Jill feel about going there?

PART D   Review Items

10. **Use the words in the box to fill in the blanks or replace the underlined words.**

eager	plain	inquire
game preserve	serve	glisten
marvelous	sober	

   a. Falling off the cliff was a <u>serious</u> experience.
   b. It was very hot so they were _____ to go swimming.
   c. It was a <u>wonderful</u> day, without a cloud in the sky.
   d. If you want to know something you can <u>ask</u> about it.
   e. The animals were safe from hunters on the _____.

Lesson 6

PART A — Word Lists

1	2	3 Vocabulary words	4 Vocabulary words
people	pressure	1. sober	1. in spite of
terrible	shriek	2. mass	2. attic
tinkle	whirlwinds	3. merrily	3. rust
sprinkle	grownups	4. wail	4. horizon
	surroundings	5. cradle	5. mile

PART B — Word Endings

- Add **ly** to each word. Remember to change the spelling of words that end in **y.**
  - happy   happi ly

1. angry
2. easy
3. tight
4. lucky
5. peaceful
6. entire
7. merry

PART C — Story Items

8. **a.** What is the name of the novel you are reading?
   b. Who is the author of that book?
   c. What is the title of the first chapter?
   d. What main thing does that chapter tell about?
9. Why was Dorothy's house small?
10. What was the name of the small hole under the middle of the floor?
11. **a.** Could Dorothy go swimming in the late summer?
    b. Tell why.
12. Name **four** things that people didn't have one hundred years ago.
13. The novel you are starting takes place in Kansas many years ago.
    a. How many states were in the United States then?
    b. During late summer there was very little water in Kansas. Why?

PART D — Review Items

14. **Use the words in the box to fill in the blanks or replace the underlined words.**

prepared	move	party
emeralds	sober	mile
running		

   a. They had a large <u>celebration</u> for his birthday.
   b. They tried to make her move, but she wouldn't <u>budge</u>.
   c. The deer went <u>bounding</u> through the forest.
   d. Maria did not have her swimsuit, so she was not _____ to go swimming.

PART E — Writing Assignment

Write a paragraph that describes what Dorothy's house looks like. Be sure the paragraph answers the following questions:
- What is the house made of?
- What color is the house?
- How many rooms does the house have?
- What furniture does the house have?

Make your paragraph at least **four** sentences long.

Lesson 7

PART A — Word Lists

1
accidents
dismally
gorgeous
sorceress
magician
deaf

2
bowed
danger
hollow

3
Vocabulary words
1. for
2. prairie
3. cyclone
4. orphan
5. rubies

4
Vocabulary words
1. deaf
2. ripples
3. brilliant
4. bondage
5. dismally

PART B

Vocabulary Sentences

1. The wind shrieked so loudly that she nearly became <u>deaf</u>.
   - happy
   - unable to hear
   - blind
2. The wind made waves and <u>ripples</u> in the grass.
   - small waves
   - bricks
   - dandelions
3. The <u>brilliant</u> feathers of the birds were every color you could imagine.
   - gray
   - bright and colorful
   - unhappy
4. We are grateful because you set us free from <u>bondage</u>.
   - slavery
   - riches
   - having fun
5. The lonely dog put his cold little nose into her face and whined <u>dismally</u>.
   - sadly
   - eagerly
   - rapidly

PART C — Word Endings

- Add **ly** to each word. Remember to change the spelling of words that end in **y**.
  - hungry   hungri ly

1. angry
2. careful
3. hearty
4. pretty
5. certain
6. ordinary
7. clear

PART D — Story Items

8. a. What is the title of the novel you are reading?
   b. Who is the author of the novel?
   c. What is the title of the second chapter?
   d. What main thing does that chapter tell about?
9. Was Uncle Henry and Aunt Em's house in the eye of the cyclone?

10. When Dorothy was rocked gently, she felt like
    - a baby in a cradle.
    - a person in a bed.
    - a baby on a rocking horse.
11. What part of Toto was sticking up through the hole?
12. Why did Dorothy close the trapdoor?
13. What did Dorothy think would happen to her if the house fell?
14. After hours passed, Dorothy calmed down and decided to
    - look out the window and find out where she was.
    - wait calmly and see what would happen.
    - make Toto feel calm.
15. At last Dorothy crawled across the floor.
    a. Where did she go?
    b. What did Dorothy do when she got to that place?

PART E   Review Items

16. **Use the words in the box to fill in the blanks or replace the underlined words.**

celebration	lantern	snarling
eagerly	mile	budge
peg		

a. Billie held the bright <u>lamp that burns oil</u> over her head.

b. She was afraid of the _____ dogs.

c. They pushed against the rock and tried to make it <u>move</u>.

d. A _____ is a long distance.

PART F   Writing Assignment

Write a paragraph about the brave things Dorothy did. Be sure the paragraph answers the following questions:
- What did Dorothy do when Toto ran away?
- How did Dorothy act while the house was spinning around?
- What did Dorothy do when Toto fell through the hole?

Make your paragraph at least **four** sentences long.

Lesson 8

PART A   Word Lists

1
wizard
messenger
gracious
civilized
leather
balanced
calmly

2
bowed
magician
jolt
handkerchief
sunbonnet

3
grownups
polished
Munchkins
paused
magic
magical

4
Vocabulary words
1. ripples
2. deaf
3. dismally
4. brilliant
5. bondage
6. inquired

5
Vocabulary words
1. cheering
2. balanced
3. for
4. rubies
5. emeralds
6. diamonds

6
Vocabulary words
1. messenger
2. civilized
3. gorgeous
4. brook
5. sprinkled
6. sorceress

PART B
Vocabulary Sentences

1. A <u>messenger</u> came to me and brought me the news.
   - thought
   - person who delivers messages
   - person who can't move

2. There are no witches in the great <u>civilized</u> countries.
   - well-mannered   • make-believe
   - unimportant

3. Everything was beautiful, especially the <u>gorgeous</u> flowers.
   - very pretty   • very loud
   - very ugly

4. The <u>brook</u> was filled with bubbling, sparkling water that rushed along.
   - small croak   • small stream
   - small puddle

5. Her white dress was <u>sprinkled</u> with bright little stars.
   - dotted   • blackened   • rough

6. She was such a powerful witch that people said she was the greatest <u>sorceress</u> in the land.
   - tree   • magician   • man

PART C   Word Endings

- Add **ly** to each word. Remember to change the spelling of words that end in **y**.

1. awful
2. heavy
3. natural
4. lucky
5. merry
6. hearty
7. serious
8. ordinary

PART D   Story Items

9. a. What is the name of the men in the picture?
   b. What is the color of their clothes?
   c. The Munchkins lived in the Land of the
      - North   ● South
      - East   ● West

d. The older woman who met Dorothy was
   - a good witch   ● a bad witch
e. She was from the Land of the
   ● North   ● South
   ● East   ● West
f. What is the name of the older woman?
g. What is the color of her clothes?
h. What did she think Dorothy was?

10. a. The witch that had been killed was from the Land of the
      ● North   ● South
      ● East   ● West
    b. The witch that had been killed was
      ● a good witch   ● a bad witch

11. **Write the correct choice on your paper.**
    a. The Wicked Witch had held all the Munchkins in _____ for many years.
       ● chains   ● bondage
       ● cellars
    b. What did the Munchkins have to do for the Wicked Witch?
       ● Paint everything green
       ● Do some jobs
       ● Slave for her night and day

12. Something happened to set the Munchkins free from bondage. What happened?

13. The Witch of the North had not set the Munchkins free because
    ● she was not a friend of the Munchkins.
    ● she was not from the Land of the East.
    ● she was not as powerful as the Witch of the East.

14. There were no witches in civilized countries.
    a. Were there any witches in Kansas?
    b. Tell why.
    c. Why were there witches in Oz?

15. a. What is the name of the Great Wizard?
    b. In what city does he live?

PART E   Review Items

16. Use the words in the box to fill in the blanks or replace the underlined words.

bounding	happily	orphan
marvelous	cyclone	peg
	slavery	

a. The slaves were kept in <u>bondage</u>.
b. If you have no parents you are an
   _____ .
c. The baby laughed <u>merrily</u>.
d. The _____ <u>blew</u> all the
   leaves off the trees.

PART F   Writing Assignment

Write a paragraph that compares Kansas with the Land of Oz. Be sure the paragraph answers the following questions:
● What does Kansas look like?
● What does the Land of Oz look like?
● What kind of people live in Kansas?
● What kind of people live in Oz?

Make your paragraph at least **four** sentences long.

Lesson 9

PART A   Word Lists

1
desert
Quadlings
Gillikins
solemn
delicious
journey
gingham

2
gracious
handkerchief
exactly
magical
Winkies
sunbonnet

3
Vocabulary words
1. gorgeous
2. messenger
3. civilized
4. sprinkled
5. brook

4
Vocabulary words
1. gingham
2. velvet
3. silk
4. leather

5
Vocabulary words
1. balanced
2. delicious
3. slate
4. pave
5. apparent

6
Vocabulary words
1. solemn
2. charm
3. sob
4. journey
5. injured
6. trot
7. brisk

PART B
Vocabulary Sentences

1. She looked very serious as she counted in a <u>solemn</u> voice.
   ● clear   ● serious   ● happy
2. Her shoes had a secret <u>charm</u> that kept her out of danger.
   ● shoelaces   ● magic power
   ● hat band
3. Dorothy began to <u>sob</u> and large tears fell from her eyes.
   ● cry   ● smile   ● listen
4. It was a long <u>journey</u> through the forest and past the fields.
   ● turkey   ● moment   ● trip
5. She fell down and <u>injured</u> her knee.
   ● hurt   ● tickled   ● listened to
6. The dog's legs were so short that he had to <u>trot</u> to keep up with his master.
   ● sleep   ● run slowly   ● eat
7. She walked at such a <u>brisk</u> pace that she arrived at the city an hour before the others.
   ● slow   ● happy   ● fast

PART C   Story Items

1. **a.** What is the title of the novel you are reading?
   b. Who is the author of that novel?
   c. What is the title of the fourth chapter?
   d. What main thing does that chapter tell about?
2. Dorothy was anxious to get back to some people.
   a. Name those two people.
   b. What would Dorothy have to cross to leave the Land of Oz?
   c. Could anyone cross that place?
3. Dorothy had the shoes that belonged to the Witch of the
   * North   * South
   * East   * West
4. **a.** Dorothy was kissed by the Witch of the
   * North   * South
   * East   * West
   b. Where did she kiss Dorothy?
   c. What did the kiss leave?
5. **a.** Which road did Dorothy take?
   b. What noise did her shoes make on that road?
   c. Would her old shoes have made that noise?

PART D   Review Items

6. You are in the Emerald City. Name the people you would reach if you went to
   a. the Land of the North.
   b. the Land of the West.
   c. the Land of the East.
   d. the Land of the South.
7. Write where Dorothy saw each thing. Choose from **Kansas** or the **Land of Oz.**
   a. A good witch   **e.** Gorgeous flowers
   b. Aunt Em   **f.** Gray grass
   c. Munchkin men   **g.** Silver shoes
   d. Funny hats   **h.** Large trees

8. Use the words in the box to fill in the blanks or replace the underlined words.

brilliant	orphan
diamonds	prairie
dismally	wail
snarling	sober

   a. The light was so _____ they couldn't look at it.
   b. The mother heard the baby's <u>howl</u> and knew it was hungry.
   c. Andrea was an _____ and couldn't remember her parents.
   d. The cowboys got on their horses and rode off across the <u>grassland with few trees.</u>
   e. When the little girl knew she was lost, she began to cry <u>sadly.</u>

PART E   Writing Assignment

Where would you rather live, in Kansas or the Land of Oz? Write a paragraph that explains your answer. Be sure the paragraph answers the following questions:
* What is good about each place?
* What is bad about each place?
* Where would you rather live and why?

Make your paragraph at least **four** sentences long.

Lesson 10

PART A   Word Lists

1
curiosity
Boq
clumsiness

2
earnestly
politely
gratefully
apparently

3
secret
scarecrow
embarrassed
uncomfortable

4
Vocabulary words
1. brisk
2. injured
3. solemn
4. trot
5. journey

5
Vocabulary words
1. field of grain
2. apparent
3. crops
4. dome
5. fiddlers

6
Vocabulary words
1. leather
2. velvet
3. gingham
4. silk

7
Vocabulary words
1. hearty
2. amused
3. resolved
4. represented
5. earnestly
6. husky
7. suspected

PART B
Vocabulary Sentences

1. Dorothy was so hungry that she ate a <u>hearty</u> supper.
   - tiny   • late   • large
2. The dog looked so funny that she <u>amused</u> all of us.
   - saddened   • bit   • entertained
3. Although he felt like crying, he <u>resolved</u> to keep the tears back.
   - made his bed   • made up his mind
   - made a mistake
4. The mask that she wore <u>represented</u> the face of a gorilla.
   - looked like   • sounded like
   - listened to
5. She wanted them to understand, so she told about her problem very <u>earnestly</u>.
   - sincerely   • happily   • timidly
6. He was a big man and he spoke in a <u>husky</u> voice.
   - small   • high   • deep or thick
7. He wasn't sure, but he <u>suspected</u> that she was a witch.
   - thought   • suspended   • knew

PART C   Story Items

1. Dorothy had shoes that belonged to the Witch of the _____.
2. **a.** Dorothy was kissed by the Witch of the
     - North   • South
     - East   • West
   b. What did that kiss leave on Dorothy's forehead?
3. **a.** What was the Munchkins' favorite color?
   b. Dorothy saw things that were that color. Name **two** things.
   c. What was the color of things in Kansas?
4. The people bowed to Dorothy because everybody knew that
   - she had come from Kansas.
   - she had received a kiss from a good witch.
   - she had destroyed the evil witch.
5. Boq and his friends had gathered to
   - celebrate the new year.
   - celebrate their freedom from bondage.
   - work in the fields together.
6. **a.** Which **two** colors did Dorothy's dress have?
   b. Which color showed that she was a witch?
   c. Which color showed that she was friendly to Munchkins?
   d. So what kind of witch did Boq think Dorothy was?
7. How many days will it take Dorothy to get to the Emerald City?
   - many   • four   • two
   - nobody knows

8. a. Who did Dorothy see in the cornfield?
  b. What was that character stuffed with that made him so light?
  c. What did he want from Oz?
  d. Could you hurt that character by stepping on his toes?
  e. Tell why.
  f. What was the only thing that character feared?
  g. Why do you think he feared that thing?

PART D
Writing Assignment

Write a paragraph that explains how the Scarecrow could help Dorothy on her journey. Be sure the paragraph answers the following questions:
- How could the Scarecrow entertain Dorothy?
- What could the Scarecrow do if Dorothy were in danger?
- How else could the Scarecrow help Dorothy?

Make your paragraph at least **four** sentences long.

Lesson 11

PART A   Word Lists

1
shoulder
inconvenient
one-legged
fortunate

2
husky
hearty
ordinary
curiosity
dreary

3
Vocabulary words
1. people of flesh and blood
2. spoil
3. husky
4. earnestly
5. suspected
6. hearty
7. represent
8. resolved

4
Vocabulary words
1. clumsiness
2. fortunate
3. dreary

PART B
Vocabulary Sentences

1. He kept falling down but he laughed at his own <u>clumsiness</u>.
   - gracefulness   ● awkwardness
   - skill
2. After they were saved from the witch they all felt <u>fortunate</u> to be alive.
   - lucky   ● sober   ● disappointed
3. Our homes were gray and very <u>dreary</u> looking.
   - dull   ● happy   ● beautiful

PART C
Reading Checkout Rules

1. If I read the passage in less than one minute, I get points as follows:
   No errors—3 points.
   1 or 2 errors—1 point.
   More than 2 errors—no points.
2. If I take more than one minute to read the passage, I get no points. But I will reread the passage until I can read it in one minute with no more than 2 errors.
3. I will write the number of points I earn in the checkout box for today's lesson.

PART D   Story Items

1. What is the title of Chapter 6?
2. a. Was the Scarecrow ever hungry?
   b. What would happen if the Scarecrow cut a hole in his mouth?
3. a. Whose shoes was Dorothy wearing?
   b. Who kissed Dorothy?
   c. What did that kiss leave on Dorothy's forehead?
      - a clear spot   - a big red mark
      - a round, shining mark
4. a. What was the Scarecrow stuffed with?
   b. What did the Scarecrow want from Oz?
   c. What was the Scarecrow afraid of?
   d. Why was the Scarecrow afraid of that?

PART E   Review Items

5. a. Where did Dorothy live before she came to the Land of Oz?
   b. Who did Dorothy live with?
   c. What carried Dorothy's house to the Land of Oz?
   d. What was the color of things where Dorothy lived?
6. a. What was the Munchkins' favorite color?
   b. What color did witches wear?
7. Name the direction you have to go from the Emerald City to reach each of these people:
   a.   the Gillikins   c.   the Winkies
   b.   the Munchkins   d.   the Quadlings
8. Write which character said each sentence. Choose between **Dorothy** and the **Scarecrow.**
   a. "I cannot understand why you want to leave this beautiful country and go back to the dry, gray place you call Kansas."
   b. "There is no place like home."
   c. "It is fortunate for Kansas that you have brains."
   d. "We people of flesh and blood would rather live there than in any other country, no matter how beautiful it is."

9. Use the words in the box to fill in the blanks or replace the underlined words.

balanced	orphan	brilliant
very pretty	rubies	cyclone
magician	move	dismally
civilized		

a. They built a huge fire that cast a <u>bright and colorful</u> light.
b. Anthony _____ the books on top of his head.
c. Suzanne was happy because her new haircut looked <u>gorgeous</u>.
d. The horses pulled and pulled but the carriage would not <u>budge</u>.
e. People who are savages are not <u>well-mannered</u>.
f. The <u>sorceress</u> waved her magic wand and changed the prince into a frog.

PART F   Writing Assignment

Do you think that the Scarecrow is smart? Write a paragraph that explains your answer. Be sure the paragraph answers the following questions:
- Why does the Scarecrow think he's stupid?
- In what ways is the Scarecrow stupid?
- In what ways is the Scarecrow smart?

Make your paragraph at least **four** sentences long.

Lesson 12

PART A   Word Lists

1
comrade
passage
companions
coward
astonished
mystery

2
fastened
embarrass
embarrassed
lifted
uplifted

3
comfort
comforted
luck
luckily
uncomfortable

4
Vocabulary words
1. fortunate
2. clumsiness
3. dreary

5
Vocabulary words
1. ray of sunshine
2. maiden
3. satisfaction
4. inconvenient
5. deserted
6. companions
7. mystery

6
Vocabulary words
1. declared
2. motionless
3. comforted

PART B
Vocabulary Sentences

1. The Scarecrow declared, "I can see quite well."
   - asked   • said   • wondered
2. She stood so still that she seemed to be motionless.
   - without movement
   - without arms
   - without a voice
3. When she rocked the baby and sang to it, the baby stopped crying and felt comforted.
   - more comfortable
   - more irritated   • worse

PART C   Story Items

1. What is the title of Chapter 7?
2. a. How long had the Scarecrow been alive?
   b. What does he know about things before that time?
   c. Who made the Scarecrow?
3. The Scarecrow felt proud when his head was fastened on.
   a. Why did he feel proud?
   - At first, the crows stayed away from the Scarecrow.
   b. What did the crows think the Scarecrow was?
   - Later, an old crow landed on the Scarecrow's shoulder.
   c. What did the old crow think the Scarecrow was?
   - The old crow said the Scarecrow could become a man if he got something.
   d. What did the Scarecrow need to get?
   e. Did the Scarecrow agree with the old crow?
4. a. What time of day was it when the travelers came to the forest?
   b. Who couldn't see in the dark?
   c. Who could see in the dark?
5. a. Where did the travelers spend the night?
   - The Scarecrow stood up in a corner while Dorothy slept.
   b. Why did he do that?
6. a. Who was making the groaning sound?
   b. How long had he been groaning?

7. Write which character said each sentence. Choose from the **farmer,** the **old crow,** or the **Scarecrow.**
  a. "My life has been so short that I really don't know anything."
  b. "How do you like those eyes?"
  c. "I felt very proud, for I thought I was as good a man as anyone."
  d. "I wonder if that farmer thought he could fool me by putting you here."
  e. "This fellow will scare the crows."
  f. "It is such an uncomfortable feeling to know that I am a fool."

PART D Review Items

8. Here are the titles of some chapters you have read:
  ● The Forest
  ● The Yellow Brick Road
  ● The Scarecrow
  Write the title of the chapter for each event.
  a. Dorothy heard a Scarecrow say, "Good day."
  b. Dorothy tried on the silver shoes.
  c. Dorothy heard a groan.
  d. The Scarecrow decided to go to see Oz.
  e. A good witch gave Dorothy a kiss.
  f. The Scarecrow told Dorothy his story.

9. Use the words in the box to fill in the blanks or replace the underlined words.

brisk	injured	lantern
trip	balanced	delicious
trot	sprinkled	apparent
serious	prairie	

  a. The ceiling was <u>dotted</u> with shining jewels.
  b. The dog was not <u>hurt</u> when the car hit it.
  c. After waiting a half hour it was _____ he wasn't coming.
  d. Mark was in a hurry so he worked at a <u>fast</u> pace.
  e. The apes thought the bananas were _____ .
  f. They packed up their suitcases because they were going on a <u>journey.</u>
  g. The bad news made them very <u>solemn.</u>
  h. Vanessa wanted to go faster so she started to <u>run slowly.</u>

PART E Writing Assignment

Write a paragraph that tells the story of the Scarecrow's life. Be sure the paragraph answers the following questions:
  ● Who made the Scarecrow and why?
  ● When did the Scarecrow begin to see and hear the world?
  ● What did the old crow tell the Scarecrow?
  ● What did the Scarecrow decide to do?

Lesson 13

PART A   Word Lists

1
shiver
jagged
sorrow
courage
guide
approve
awkward

2
marriage
cruel
halves
alas

3
Vocabulary words
1. comforted
2. motionless
3. inconvenient
4. declared
5. deserted
6. maiden
7. satisfaction

4
Vocabulary words
1. courage
2. awkward
3. jagged
4. moved

5
Vocabulary words
1. shouldered his axe
2. comrade
3. passage
4. misfortune

PART B

Vocabulary Sentences

1. The woodman <u>shouldered his axe</u> and marched through the forest.
   - brought his axe to his shoulder
   - thought his axe was his shoulder
   - made his axe look like a shoulder
2. They met a <u>comrade</u> who joined them on their journey.
   - enemy   • tree   • friend
3. The woodman cleared a <u>passage</u> through the thick shrubs and bushes.
   - passenger   • idea   • path
4. The woman had the <u>misfortune</u> of cutting her leg with her axe.
   - good luck   • bad luck   • blade

PART C   Story Items

1. What is the Title of Chapter 8?
2. When Dorothy found the Tin Woodman, he could not move.
   a. Why couldn't he move?
   b. What did Dorothy get for the Tin Woodman?
   c. Where did Dorothy oil the Tin Woodman?
   d. What could make the Tin Woodman rust again?
3. a. Who did the Tin Woodman want to marry?
   - The Munchkin girl
   - An old woman
   - The Wicked Witch
   b. Who did not want the Tin Woodman to get married?
   - The Munchkin girl
   - An old woman
   - The Wicked Witch
   c. Who put a spell on the Tin Woodman's axe?

4. The axe cut off the Tin Woodman's legs, arms, head, and body.
   a. Who made new parts for the Woodman?
   b. What metal were those parts made of?
   c. What was the Woodman's new body missing?
   d. Did the Woodman still love the Munchkin girl?
5. a. What did Dorothy want from Oz?
   b. What did the Scarecrow want from Oz?
   c. What did the Tin Woodman want from Oz?
   d. What would the Tin Woodman do if Oz gave him what he wanted?

PART D   Review Items

6. You are in the Emerald City. Name the people you would reach if you went to
   a. the Land of the South.
   b. the Land of the East.
   c. the Land of the West.
   d. the Land of the North.

7. Use the words in the box to fill in the blanks or replace the underlined words.

entertained	balanced
looked like	injured
made up her mind	suspected
gorgeous	solemn
sorceress	crops
apparent	

a. They laughed because they were <u>amused</u>.

b. The colors of the sunset were <u>very pretty</u>.

c. The farmer picked his _____ .

d. She held a tray in each hand and carefully _____ them.

e. She <u>resolved</u> that she would do a better job the next time.

f. She made a few lines that <u>represented</u> a horse.

g. When the people went to work they looked very <u>serious</u>.

h. He <u>thought</u> that the man was lying.

PART E   Writing Assignment

Write a paragraph that explains how the Woodman became the Tin Woodman. Be sure the paragraph answers the following questions:

- Who did the Woodman want to marry?
- Who put a spell on the Woodman's axe and why?
- What did the axe do to the Woodman?
- Who repaired the Woodman?

Lesson 14

PART A   Word Lists

1	2	3	4	5 Vocabulary words	6 Vocabulary words
peculiar	hinges	here	guide	1. comrade	1. approve of
manage	places	hereafter	welcome	2. passage	2. sorrow
Kalidahs	fences	bearable	ashamed	3. misfortune	3. unbearable
fierce	cottages	unbearable	dangerous		4. astonished
relief	manages				5. remarkable
adventure					6. shiver
disease					7. coward
					8. strides

PART B   Vocabulary Sentences

1. Toto did not <u>approve of</u> the new comrade and tried to bite him.
   - smell   • look at   • like

2. When his friends left, he felt great <u>sorrow</u> and started to cry.
   - happiness   • anger   • sadness

3. When she couldn't stand being alone any more, she cried, "This is <u>unbearable</u>."
   - something I don't mind
   - something I can't stand
   - something I like

4. When she saw the Scarecrow wink at her, she was <u>astonished</u>.
   - not interested   • surprised
   - hopeful

5. The dog was <u>remarkable</u> because it had a coat of seven different colors.
   - ordinary   • boring   • unusual

6. When she went outside without a coat on, she began to <u>shiver</u> from the cold.
   - tremble and vibrate
   - run and jump   • sweat and pant

7. He was such a <u>coward</u> that he would pick on very little people, but he was afraid of everybody else.
   - brave person   • chicken
   - nice person

8. The Lion's <u>strides</u> were so long that he took one step each time Dorothy took three steps.
   - steps   • windows   • hooves

PART C Story Items

1. What is the title of Chapter 9?
2. What kind of place were the travelers walking through in Chapter 9?
3. The Lion attacked the travelers.
   a. Who did the Lion knock over easily?
   b. Who nearly ruined the Lion's claws?
   c. Who slapped the Lion on the nose?
4. Dorothy told the Lion that he was a big _____.
5. a. A lion is supposed to act
   - cowardly   - bravely
   - politely   - anxiously
   b. The Lion is supposed to be the King of _____.
6. a. What did the Lion do to make other animals run away?
   b. But what would have happened if those animals had tried to fight the Lion?
7. a. What did the Lion want to get from Oz?
   b. What did the Scarecrow want to get from Oz?
   c. What did the Tin Woodman want to get from Oz?
   d. What did Dorothy want to get from Oz?
8. a. What did the Tin Woodman do after he stepped on the beetle?
   b. What happened to the Tin Woodman's jaws when he did that?
   c. Who figured out how to fix the Tin Woodman?
   d. What did that character use to fix the Tin Woodman?

PART D Review Items

9. Write which character said each sentence. Choose from **Dorothy**, the **Scarecrow**, the **Tin Woodman**, or the **Lion**.
   a. "I am not afraid so long as I have my oilcan."
   b. "Don't you dare bite Toto."
   c. "I know that I am a coward."
   d. "All the other animals expect me to be brave."

e. "I cannot have heart disease."
f. "My life is unbearable without a bit of courage."
g. "There is no place like home."
h. "I am afraid of a lighted match."

10. Some of the travelers do **not** eat or sleep.
   a. Write the names of the travelers who do **not** get tired or thirsty.
   b. Write the names of the travelers who must sleep.
   c. Write the names of the travelers who do **not** have to eat.
   d. Write the names of the travelers who must eat.

11. **Use the words in the box to fill in the blanks or replace the underlined words.**

represented	merrily
sprinkled	hurt
apparent	husky
delicious	orphan
thought	

   a. Jean put spoonful after spoonful of the _____ ice cream in her mouth.
   b. Karen saw the clouds and suspected it was going to rain.
   c. When the dog wouldn't eat, it was _____ to Don that he was sick.
   d. Cavemen paintings looked like the animals they hunted.
   e. Jim was injured when he fell off his bike.
   f. Chan was a big man and he spoke in a _____ voice.

PART E Writing Assignment

Write a paragraph that describes the Lion. Be sure the paragraph answers the following questions:
- Is the Lion brave or cowardly?
- How does the Lion scare other animals?
- What would happen if the other animals tried to fight the Lion?
- What does the Lion want and why?

Lesson 15

PART A Word Lists

1	2	3
distances	adventure	faintest
edges	delight	shaggy
cottages	delightful	relief
fences	fierce	Kalidahs
places		

4
Vocabulary words
1. approve of
2. sorrow
3. unbearable
4. strides
5. astonished
6. remarkable
7. awkward
8. jagged

5
Vocabulary words
1. snug
2. crouch
3. gloomy

6
Vocabulary words
1. splendid
2. peculiar
3. dreadful

PART B

Vocabulary Sentences

1. Dorothy built a <u>splendid</u> fire that made large flames and gave off a lot of heat.
   - ugly   • marvelous   • small
2. They saw <u>peculiar</u> looking people who had three eyes and four arms.
   - ordinary   • regular   • strange
3. When she saw the horrible things the tigers did, she said, "Those beasts are <u>dreadful</u>."
   - horrible   • great   • silly

PART C Story Items

1. What is the title of Chapter 10?
2. The travelers camped out under a large tree. How much food did Dorothy have after she and Toto ate the bread?
3. The Lion offered to get some food for Dorothy. How was the Lion going to do that?
4. **Write the missing words on your paper.**
   The Tin Woodman didn't want the Lion to get that food because the Tin Woodman would start to _____ and then parts of his body would _____.
5. The Scarecrow stayed away from the fire. Why did the Scarecrow do that?

6. **Look at the picture and answer the questions.**
   - The ditch blocked the road.
   a. Why didn't the travelers climb down the ditch?
   b. Who figured out how to get across the ditch?
   - As part of the plan, the Lion had to do something.
   c. What did the Lion have to do?
   d. How did the other travelers get across the ditch?

7. a. Who came up with a plan for getting across the next ditch?
   b. Who chopped down the tree?
   c. Who made sure the tree fell across the ditch?

8. The Kalidahs chased the travelers across the tree.
   a. The Kalidahs had a body like a _____ and a head like a _____.
   b. What kind of claws did the Kalidahs have?

9. a. What did the Lion do when the Kalidahs appeared?
   b. Then the Kalidahs
      - stopped for an instant and continued.
      - turned around and left.
      - didn't even pause for a second.

10. a. Who came up with a plan to stop the Kalidahs?
    b. What was that plan?
    c. What happened to the Kalidahs?

PART D   Review Items

11. Write the direction you have to go from the Emerald City to reach each of these people:
    a. the Quadlings   c. the Munchkins
    b. the Winkies   d. the Gillikins

12. Write whether each sentence tells about **Kansas,** the **Land of the Munchkins,** or the **Forest.**
    a. The wind howled across the prairie.
    b. The sun baked the land into a gray mass.
    c. There were neat blue fences beside the road.
    d. The road was covered with branches.
    e. There were deep ditches with ragged rocks on the bottom.

13. Here are the titles of some chapters you have read:

- Kansas
- The Kalidahs
- The Tin Woodman

Write the title of the chapter for each event.

  a. The Lion roared at two great beasts.
  b. The Tin Woodman tells his story.
  c. Uncle Henry looked anxiously at the sky.
  d. The country was gray and the land was cracked.
  e. Dorothy found a can with oil in it.

14. Use the words in the box to fill in the blanks or to replace the underlined words.

mystery	satisfaction
amused	suspected
solemn	looked like
companion	civilized

a. The clown <u>entertained</u> them.
b. The five-pointed object <u>represented</u> a star.
c. After completing the climb, she felt great _____.
d. The cat was her only _____.
e. The strange noises in the house at night were a _____ to them.

PART E   Writing Assignment

Do you think the Tin Woodman really needs a heart? Write a paragraph that explains your answer. Be sure the paragraph answers the following questions:

- Why doesn't the Tin Woodman have a heart now?
- What does the Tin Woodman think will happen when he gets a heart?
- Does the Tin Woodman act like someone without a heart? Why or why not?

Make your paragraph at least **four** sentences long.

Lesson 16

PART A   Word Lists

1
beckon
scent
curtsy
hurriedly

2
downstream
cornfield
harmless
wildcat
indeed
hereafter

3
adventure
fastened
dismal
dismally

4
Vocabulary words
1. raft
2. meadow
3. cozy
4. cluster
5. scarlet
6. dazzle
7. scarcely

5
Vocabulary words
1. delightful
2. refreshed
3. glare

PART B
Vocabulary Sentences

1. They were pleased to see this <u>delightful</u> meadow before them.
   - ugly   - wonderful   - sad
2. The next morning, Dorothy said, "I feel great. The long sleep made me feel <u>refreshed</u>."
   - tired   - lonesome
   - full of energy
3. The <u>glare</u> of the lights almost blinded her.
   - sound   - feeling   - brightness

PART C   Story Items

1. What did the travelers come upon in the afternoon?

2. **a.** Who figured out a way to get across the river?
   b. What was his plan?
   c. Who built the raft?

3. **Look at the picture and answer the questions.**
   - The Scarecrow and the Tin Woodman are holding poles.
   a. The end of the poles are pushing against _____.
   - There are two arrows in the picture.
   b. Which arrow shows the direction the current is moving—Arrow A or Arrow B?
   c. Which arrow shows the direction the raft is moving?

4. The travelers had a hard time in the middle of the river.
   a. What made the raft move downstream?
   b. Why couldn't the poles reach the bottom anymore?
   c. As the raft floated downstream it went farther and farther from the _____.

5. The Scarecrow pushed extra hard on his pole.
   a. What happened to the end of the pole?
   b. Did the Scarecrow hang onto the other end?
   c. What did the raft keep doing?

   d. So where did that leave the Scarecrow?
   e. Was this the first time the Scarecrow had been stuck on a pole?
   f. Where was the Scarecrow the first time he was on a pole?

PART D   Study Skills

6. **Find the following words in your glossary. Copy what the glossry says about each word.**
   a. grate
   b. parlor

PART E   Review Items

7. **Use the words in the box to fill in the blanks or replace the underlined words.**

husky	declared	suspected
dull	clumsiness	deserted
coward	fortunate	inconvenient
gorgeous	comforted	

   a. The stranger went exactly where she thought he would go.
   b. The clown amused everybody with his awkwardness.
   c. It was lucky that the bus hadn't left without her.

d. The rainy day looked very <u>dreary</u> and gray.

e. Losing all the papers he had written was most <u>annoying</u>.

f. Carlos spoke loudly when he <u>said</u> that he was quitting his job.

g. The sound of the ocean _____ her and she fell asleep.

h. Diego was _____ and sat sadly in the parking lot.

PART F   Writing Assignment

The travelers are still floating downstream. Write a story that tells what you think will happen next. Be sure the story answers the following questions:
- What will happen to the Scarecrow?
- What will happen to the other travelers?

Lesson 17

PART A   Word Lists

1	2	3	4
spicy	shallow	**Vocabulary words**	**Vocabulary words**
odor	blossoms	1. beckon	1. fond of
mistress	carpet	2. dazzle	2. scent, odor
	poison	3. scarlet	3. mistress
	poisonous	4. cluster	4. shrill
		5. scarcely	5. timid
		6. dreadful	6. permit
		7. refreshed	7. curtsy
		8. glare	8. spicy
		9. delightful	9. therefore

PART B   Story Items

1. At the beginning of Chapter 12, the raft was still floating downstream.
   a. What made the raft float downstream?
   b. Who pulled the raft toward the shore?
   c. After the travelers reached the shore, they decided to walk back to the _____.
   d. On their way, they saw the _____ in the middle of the river.

2. a. What kind of bird carried the Scarecrow back to the shore?
   b. Why was it so easy for the bird to lift the Scarecrow?

3. a. What color are the flowers?
   b. What happens when you breathe their odor?
   c. What could happen to you if you were not carried away from the flowers?

4. The Scarecrow and the Tin Woodman are carrying Dorothy away from the flowers.
   a. Where will they put her?
   b. What is the air like in that spot?
   c. So what will happen to Dorothy?
   d. Can the Tin Woodman and the Scarecrow carry the Lion?
   e. So what will happen to the Lion?

5. Here are some events from Chapter 12:
   - The travelers came to a field of flowers.
   - The Stork saved the Scarecrow.
   - The Lion pulled the raft to shore.
   - The Lion fell asleep.
   - Dorothy and Toto fell asleep.
   a. Write the event that occured **first**.
   b. Write the event that occurred **last**.

PART C   Study Skills

6. **Find the following words in your glossary. Copy what the glossary says about each word.**
   a. flogged
   b. charred

You have learned how to use your glossary. You can use your glossary when you are not sure of the meaning of a word. You can also use it to correct your independent work.

PART D   Review Items

7. The characters in the story want something.
   a. Who wants to go back to Kansas?
   b. Who wants brains?
   c. Who wants a heart?
   d. Who wants courage?
8. **Use the words in the box to fill in the blanks or replace the underlined words.**

satisfaction	inconvenient
comforted	surprise
without movement	misfortune
sprinkled	deserted
remarkable	dreary
passage	comrade
sorrow	

   a. After the teacher told him to sit still, he was <u>motionless</u>.
   b. Simone held the baby and _____ him.

c. It was her <u>bad luck</u> to have no money.
d. Beverly's skirt looked faded and <u>dull</u>.
e. Someone who's your friend is your

   _____ .
f. The <u>path</u> through the forest was so narrow they could barely follow it.
g. She didn't want to do it because it was so _____ .
h. She felt <u>sadness</u> over the death of her pet.
i. The sight of the city will amaze and <u>astonish</u> you.
j. It was <u>unusual</u> that a one-legged man won the foot race.

PART E   Writing Assignment

Do you think the Lion is brave? Write a paragraph that explains your answer. Be sure the paragraph answers the following questions:
- What brave things has the Lion done since the travelers met him?
- What cowardly things has the Lion done?
- Do you think the Lion could be braver? How?

Make your paragraph at least **four** sentences long.

Lesson 18

PART A   Word Lists

1	2	3	4
majesty	beast	**Vocabulary words**	**Vocabulary words**
limbs	poisonous	1. fond of	1. stunned
introduce	manage	2. scampered off	2. drawn
harnessed	under	3. curtsy	3. dwelled
rescued	underneath	4. timid	4. presence
dwelled	hurriedly	5. shrill	5. glittered
presence	exclaimed	6. therefore	6. throne
		7. permit	7. oats

PART B Story Items

1. **a.** At the beginning of Chapter 13, what was chasing the Queen?
   b. Who saved the Queen?
   c. How many mice did the Queen command?
2. A mouse asked the Tin Woodman if they could do anything for him.
   a. Why did the mouse ask him that?
   b. Could the Tin Woodman think of anything the mice could do?
   c. Who thought of something the mice could do?
3. At first, the mice were afraid of saving the Lion.
   a. Why were the mice afraid?
   b. There was no reason for the mice to be afraid of the Lion.
   They didn't know the Lion was really a _____.
4. Here are some events from Chapter 13:
   • The mice pulled the cart.
   • The Tin Woodman chopped down some trees.
   • The Queen promised to help the travelers again.
   • The Scarecrow came up with a plan to save the Lion.
   • The Tin Woodman saved the Queen.
   a. Write the event that occurred **first.**
   b. Write the event that occurred **last.**
5. **Look at the picture and answer the questions.**
   a. Who made the cart?
   b. Where did the wheels come from?
   c. Why is the Lion asleep?
   d. The Queen is telling the mice to work quickly. Why is the Queen doing that?
6. At the end of Chapter 13, the Queen promised the travelers something.
   a. What could the travelers do if they ever needed help?
   b. Do you think the travelers will need more help sometime?

PART C Review Items

7. Write which character each sentence describes. Choose from **Dorothy, Tin Woodman, Lion** or **Scarecrow.**
   a. This character came from Kansas.
   b. This character stunned a wildcat.
   c. This character was put on a cart.
   d. This character built a raft and a cart.
   e. This character ate raw meat.
   f. This character was carried by a stork.
   g. This character was given a pair of silver shoes.
   h. This character came up with a plan to save the Lion.

8. Use the words in the box to fill in the blanks or replace the underlined words.

inconvenient	marvelous	steps
refreshed	mystery	lucky
shivered	coward	sorrow

a. The cold kitten <u>trembled and vibrated</u>.

b. The cats were <u>fortunate</u> because they were not <u>bothered</u> by dogs.

c. The Lion had no courage and was a _____.

d. Lisa ran away with long <u>strides</u>.

e. It was a <u>splendid</u> sunny morning.

f. After the dog took a nap, it felt <u>full of energy</u>.

PART D Writing Assignment

Write a paragraph that explains the Scarecrow's plan for saving the Lion. Be sure the paragraph answers the following questions:
● Who made the cart?
● How were the mice fastened to the cart?
● Why did the mice have to work quickly?
● What made the cart move?

Make your paragraph at least **four** sentences long.

Lesson 19

PART A Word Lists

1	2	3	4	5
generously	yawning	silver	**Vocabulary words**	**Vocabulary words**
cereal	shadows	silvery	1. presence	1. countless
basin	starved	guard	2. glittered	2. tint
spectacles	palace	guarded	3. dwelled	3. guardian
apron	arched	guardian		4. marble
	honest	disturbed		5. studded
	scrambled			6. admit
	ceiling			7. basin
				8. prefer
				9. spectacles

PART B Story Items

1. a. What was the color of things in the Land of the Munchkins?
   b. What is the color of things in the land the travelers are in now?
   c. What is the color of the road?
2. Why didn't anybody come out to talk to the travelers?
3. The man with the bad leg told the travelers many things about Oz.
   a. Had the man been to the Emerald City?
   b. Had the man ever seen Oz?
   c. Did the man know of anybody who had seen Oz?
4. The man said that Oz could take many forms.
   a. Name **three** forms that the man mentioned.
   b. Who knows what Oz really looks like?
5. The man said that Oz could help the travelers.
   a. Why could Oz help the Scarecrow?
   b. Why could Oz help the Tin Woodman?
   c. Why could Oz help the Lion?

6. As they were walking the next morning, the travelers saw a glow in the sky.
   a. What color was the glow?
   b. Name the place this glow came from.
   c. Surrounding this city was a large green _____ .
7. When the gate opened, the travelers saw a room.
   a. What were the walls covered with?
   b. Who was in the room?
   c. What was next to that character?

PART C   Review Items

8. Use the words in the box to fill in the blanks or replace the underlined words.

awkwardness	peculiar	comrade
dreadful	coward	crouched
declared	gloomy	snug
deserted	cozy	

   a. When the Scarecow fell down, he was not upset by his <u>clumsiness</u>.
   b. Everybody else liked Larry, but she thought he was <u>horrible</u>.
   c. She was lonely because she had been _____ .
   d. They all stared at the cat because she was so <u>strange</u> looking.
   e. The sleeping bag was warm and <u>tight-fitting</u>.
   f. When they drew near, he _____ behind a bush.
   g. The room was dark and <u>dismal</u>.
   h. With the fireplace burning, the room was very <u>comfortable</u>.

PART D   Writing Assignment

The travelers have seen a small part of the Emerald City. Write a paragraph that describes what the rest of the Emerald City might look like. Be sure the paragraph answers the following questions:
● What color is everything?
● What are the streets like?
● What are the buildings like?

Make your paragraph at least **four** sentences long.

Lesson 20

PART A   Word Lists

1	2	3	4
sunshine	cereal	uniform	**Vocabulary words**
wildcat	honest	furniture	1. guardian
woodman	ceiling	whistle	2. prefer
scarecrow	lemonade	fountain	3. basin
everything			4. studded
therefore			5. admit
			6. marble

PART B   Story Items

1. a. What did Dorothy tell the Guardian that they wanted to do?
   b. At first the Guardian was very
      * sad.   * angry.   * surprised.
      * sleepy.
2. The Guardian told the travelers what Oz might do if they wanted to see him for foolish reasons. What might he do?
3. The Guardian put spectacles on all the travelers.
   a. What color was the glass in the spectacles?
   b. What color was the Emerald City?
   c. How many people in the Emerald City wore spectacles?
4. The Guardian said that the spectacles would keep the travelers from going blind. What could blind the travelers?
5. The Guardian led the travelers through the streets of the Emerald City.
   a. What stone were the houses and sidewalks made of?
   b. What kind of gem was studded everywhere?
   c. Were there any animals?
   d. What was exactly in the middle of the city?
6. Oz agreed to see the travelers.
   a. How many of the travelers would Oz see at one time?
   b. How many would Oz see each day?
   c. Where did Dorothy and Toto stay while they were waiting to see Oz?
7. a. Which **three** travelers slept that night?
   b. Which **two** travelers did not sleep?

PART C   Review Items

8. Write whether you would see each thing in the **Emerald City,** the **Field of Flowers,** or the **River.**
   a. A room with a high arched ceiling.
   b. A group of field mice pulling a heavy cart.
   c. A swift current.

d. People wearing green spectacles.
e. A large palace.
f. A group of people on a raft.
g. Sidewalks made of marble.
h. Walls studded with emeralds.

9. **Use the words in the box to fill in the blanks or replace the underlined words.**

companion	dazzled	scarlet
inconvenient	snug	strides
fortunate	crouch	hardly
peculiar	deserted	refreshed
apparent		

   a. When Todd awoke the next morning, he felt strong and <u>full of energy.</u>
   b. Her jewels were so <u>brilliant</u> that they _____ people.
   c. When she opened the gift she realized how <u>lucky</u> she was.
   d. The man and <u>his</u> traveling _____ rode down the trail.
   e. The store was in a place that was very <u>annoying.</u>
   f. Things that are strange are _____.
   g. She was so tired that she could <u>scarcely</u> stand up.
   h. The <u>little</u> child picked five <u>red</u> roses.
   i. The doorway was so low that they had to _____ to get inside.
   j. After everyone left, she felt _____.

PART D   Writing Assignment

If you could make a city, what would it be like? Write a paragraph that explains your answer. Be sure the paragraph answers the following questions:
* What would the buildings look like?
* What kinds of stores and parks would the city have?
* How would people get from one part of the city to another?

Make your paragraph at least **four** sentences long.

Lesson 21

PART A   Word Lists

1	2	3	4
rhinoceros	enormous	giant	**Vocabulary words**
singe	tremendous	disappointed	1. enormous
grindstone	anxious	dreadfully	2. meek
	gorgeous	expect	3. weep
			4. willingly
			5. tremendous
			6. grant
			7. terror
			8. request
			9. singed

PART B   Reading Checkout Rules

1. If I read the passage in less than one minute, I get points as follows:
   No errors—3 points.
   1 or 2 errors—1 point.
   More than 2 errors—no points.
2. If I take more than one minute to read the passage, I get no points. But I will reread the passage until I can read it in one minute with no more than 2 errors.
3. I will write the number of points I earn in the checkout box for today's lesson.

PART C   Story Items

1. a. What room did Dorothy enter at the beginning of the chapter?
   b. What were the walls, ceilings, and floor covered with?
2. There was a big throne in the middle of the room.
   a. What was the throne made out of?
   b. Where was Oz?
   c. Oz was in the form of a
      - beast   - monkey   - princess
      - head
   d. What were the **two** things about Dorothy that interested Oz?
      - her hair   - her shoes
      - her dog   - the mark
3. Oz said, "Help me and I will help you."
   a. What did Dorothy want Oz to do for her?
   b. What did Oz want Dorothy to do for him?
4. Who knew how to kill the Wicked Witch of the West?
5. Here are some events from Chapter 16:
   - Dorothy entered the throne room.
   - Dorothy told Oz about the Witch of the North.
   - Dorothy told Oz that she wanted to go back to Kansas.
   - Oz told Dorothy to kill the Wicked Witch of the West.
   - Oz asked Dorothy how she got the silver shoes.
   a. Write the event that occurred **first**.
   b. Write the event that occurred **last**.

PART D   Review Items

6. Use the words in the box to fill in the blanks or replace the underlined words.

refreshed	so	cluster
wonderful	timid	dismal
dreadful	crouch	mystery
scarcely	scarlet	dazzle
smell		

a. Nobody could eat the meal because it had a <u>horrible</u> taste.
b. Carol found the book both interesting and <u>delightful</u>.
c. It was <u>so surprising</u> that they could <u>hardly</u> believe it.
d. The huge footprint in the sand was one _____ that no one could figure out.
e. The buffalo huddled together in a <u>group</u> when they saw the wolves coming.
f. Steve stared into the <u>gloomy</u> shadows of the tunnel.
g. The walk in the cold air _____ her and made her feel wide awake.
h. The bulldog put his nose to the ground and followed the <u>scent</u> of the fox.
i. The kitten was too <u>shy</u> to come out from behind the refrigerator.
j. Jack was very tired, <u>therefore</u> he went to sleep.

PART E   Writing Assignment

Write a paragraph that describes the throne room. Be sure the paragraph answers the following questions:
- What shape is the room?
- What is the room made of?
- What is in the room?

Make your paragraph at least **four** sentences long.

Lesson 22

PART A   Word Lists

1	2	3 Vocabulary words	4 Vocabulary words	5 Vocabulary words
daisies	singe	1. tremendous	1. slightest	1. pack
telescope	single	2. meek	2. kingdom	2. flock
castle	sorrowfully	3. enormous	3. grindstone	3. swarm
	rhinoceros	4. terror	4. pure	
	singed	5. singed	5. advance	
	cackle	6. request	6. scatter	
	cackling	7. grant		

PART B   Story Items

1. Oz has taken many forms.
   a. What form did Oz take for Dorothy?
   b. What form did Oz take for the Scarecrow?
   c. What form did Oz take for the Tin Woodman?
   d. What form did Oz take for the Lion?
2. Write which traveler saw each form of Oz.
   a. Something with thick and wooly hair
   b. Something with wings
   c. A head that was floating by itself
   d. Something that was very hot
   e. Something with five eyes
3. a. What did the Scarecrow ask Oz for?
   b. What did the Tin Woodman ask Oz for?
   c. What did the Lion ask Oz for?
4. a. Did Oz agree to help each traveler?
   b. But what did the traveler have to do first?

PART C   Review Items

5. Write which character each statement is about.
   a. This character didn't have the courage to kill the Witch.
   b. This character didn't have enough brains to kill the Witch.
   c. This character didn't have the heart to kill the Witch.
6. a. In which land did the Wicked Witch live?
   b. Which people lived in that land?
   c. In which direction would the travelers have to go to reach that land.
7. **Use the words in the box to fill in the blanks or replace the underlined words.**

cluster	glittered	admit
preferred	presence	permit
therefore	stunned	odor
suspected	dreary	tint
shy		

   a. They could not stand the <u>smell</u> of the garbage cans.
   b. She was the fastest runner in the race, <u>so</u> she won easily.

   c. Their mother would not _____ them to eat candy.
   d. When she walked out on the stage, everybody knew that she was not <u>timid</u>.
   e. The blow on the head _____ him for a few moments.
   f. The queen was bored and welcomed the clown's _____ .
   g. The guardian would not _____ her to the throne room.
   h. The girl ate apples, but she _____ peaches.
   i. The artist added a _____ of blue to her painting.
   j. The gold tooth <u>sparkled</u> in her mouth when she smiled.

PART D   Writing Assignment

The Wizard takes different forms. Write a paragraph that describes what he might look like if you saw him. Be sure the paragraph answers the following questions:
- What does his body look like?
- What does his voice sound like?

Make your paragraph at least **four** sentences long.

Lesson 23

PART A   Word Lists

1	2	3	4
seize	buttercups	**Vocabulary words**	**Vocabulary words**
threaten	disobey	1. advance	1. untilled
desperate	daisy	2. scatter	2. castle
rejoice	daisies	3. pure	3. strike
	hill	4. flock	4. heap
	hillier	5. swarm	5. rage
	fierce	6. pack	6. spear
			7. seize
			8. fate
			9. tempt
			10. fine

PART B   Story Items

1. The travelers started walking toward the Land of the West.
   a. Was there a road for them to walk on?
   b. Were they still wearing spectacles?
   c. What color was Dorothy's dress in the Emerald City?
   d. What color was Dorothy's dress now?
   e. Why do you think the dress changed color?
2. The Wicked Witch saw the travelers.
   a. How many eyes did the Wicked Witch have?
   b. In what way was the Witch's eye like a telescope?
   c. How did the Witch feel when she saw the travelers?
   d. What was hanging around the Witch's neck?
3. The Witch blew on her silver whistle once.
   a. Which animals came running up to her?
   b. What did she tell those animals to do?
   c. Who stunned those animals?
   d. What did he stun them with?
4. The Witch blew on her silver whistle twice.
   a. Which animals came to her that time?
   b. Who scared those animals away?
   c. To scare them away, that character went spinning around and
      • waved his arms.
      • whistled three times.
      • made a strange noise.
      • shouted loudly.
5. The Witch blew on her silver whistle three times.
   a. Which animals came to her that time?
   b. Who protected Dorothy, Toto, and the Lion from those animals?
   c. Who was the only traveler those animals attacked?
   d. Why did those animals die?

PART C   Review Items

6. Write which character could have said each sentence.
   a. "I don't have the heart to harm even a Witch."
   b. "My clothes are no longer green."
   c. "I am to afraid to kill the Witch."
   d. "Those bees will break their stingers against me."
   e. "Oz will not send me home until the Wicked Witch is dead."
   f. "Spread my straw over Dorothy, Toto, and the Lion."
7. **Use the words in the box to fill in the blanks or replace the underlined words.**

preferred	enormous
stunned	amused
glisten	journey
admitted	smell
permit	timid

   a. She held the flowers and breathed in their magnificent <u>odor</u>.
   b. The guard would not _____ anybody to go inside the city.
   c. After Rhoda was _____ to the office, she sat and waited.
   d. The boxer was <u>knocked out</u> from the punch on his jaw.
   e. The hole was so <u>huge</u> that they couldn't see the bottom.
   f. He was a <u>meek</u> little boy who never said much.
   g. Diana went to work, but she <u>would have chosen</u> to sleep.

PART D   Writing Assignment

Write a story that describes how the travelers defeated the animals sent by the Wicked Witch. Be sure the paragraph answers the following questions:
• Which animals did the Wicked Witch send?
• How did the travelers defeat each animal?

Lesson 24

PART A   Word Lists

1
seize
threatened
disobey
seized
desperate
desperately

2
chatter
invisible
struggle
strange
chattering

3
Vocabulary words
1. fate
2. seize
3. tempt

4
Vocabulary words
1. chattering
2. battered
3. bundle
4. courtyard
5. desperately
6. cunning
7. rejoice

PART B   Story Items

1. The Wicked Witch called the Monkeys.
   a. She could command the Monkeys because she owned the _____.
   b. How many times can the owner command them?
   c. How many times had the Witch already commanded them at the beginning of Chapter 19?
   d. The Witch commanded the Monkeys to destroy everybody except the _____.
   e. How were the Monkeys different from ordinary monkeys?

2. Some of the Monkeys seized the Tin Woodman.
   a. What did they drop him on?
   b. What happened to the Tin Woodman's body?

3. Some of the Monkeys caught the Scarecrow.
   a. What did the Monkeys do with the Scarecrow's straw?
   b. What did the Monkeys throw into a tree?

4. Some of the Monkeys caught the Lion.
   a. Why didn't they kill the Lion?
   b. Where did they carry the Lion?

5. The Monkeys did not harm Dorothy.
   a. How did the leader of the Monkeys know that Dorothy was protected by the Power of Good?
   b. Which power did the Monkey think was greater—The Power of Good or the Power of Evil?

6. a. What **two** things about Dorothy worried the Wicked Witch?
   b. Who else had been interested in those two things?
   c. Did Dorothy know about the power of the shoes?

7. What room did the Witch order Dorothy to work in?

8. a. What character did the Witch put in her courtyard?
   b. When that character did not obey the Witch, she decided to
      • beat him.
      • put him in the castle.
      • throw him in the river.
      • starve him.
   c. Why didn't that character starve to death?

9. Why didn't the Witch bleed?

PART C   Review Items

10. a. What color was everything near the Emerald City?
    b. What color was everything in the Land of the Munchkins?
    c. What color was everything in the Land of the Winkies?

11. Use the words in the box to fill in the blanks or replace the underlined words.

splendid	presence	permit
timid	tremendous	great fear
cry	asked for	motionless
shrill	dwelled	singed

a. When Elsa tried to sing the high note, her voice became very _____.

b. The cat was nervous in the _____ of the dog.

c. The witch would not _____ them to eat candy.

d. A strange sorceress <u>lived</u> in the gloomy castle.

e. The sad woman started to <u>weep</u>.

f. There was a <u>great</u> explosion that shook the building.

g. When the lion stepped from the shadows, the man's eyes grew wide with <u>terror</u>.

h. She tried to be polite when she <u>requested</u> a clean bowl.

i. The dog's whiskers were <u>slightly burned</u> by the fire.

PART D   Writing Assignment

What powerful charm do you think the silver shoes have? Write a paragraph that explains your answer. Be sure the paragraph answers the following questions:

- How can you make the charm work?
- What happens when you use the charm?

Make your paragraph at least **four** sentences long.

Lesson 25

PART A   Word Lists

1	2	3	4
anxious	holiday	**Vocabulary words**	**Vocabulary words**
gorgeous	despair	1. cunning	1. cruelty
enormous	desperate	2. rejoice	2. feast
tremendous	straightened	3. desperately	3. tenderly
	despairing		4. mend
	invisible		
	bathe		
	bathing		

PART B   Story Items

1. What **two** things was the Witch afraid of?

2. a. Why did the Witch want the silver shoes?

  b. Why didn't she take them when Dorothy was asleep?

  c. Why didn't she take them when Dorothy was bathing?

3. a. Who put an iron bar in the middle of the kitchen floor?

  b. What was unusual about that bar?

  c. Who tripped over the bar?

  d. What did she lose when she tripped over the bar?

4. Dorothy became very angry with the Witch.

  a. What did Dorothy throw at the Witch?

  b. What happened to the Witch?

5. Dorothy had set the Winkies free from bondage.

  a. Who else had Dorothy set free from bondage?

  b. What color did the Winkies wear?

6. The Winkies helped Dorothy rescue the Tin Woodman and the Scarecrow.

  a. What was wrong with the Tin Woodman's body?

b. Who fixed the Tin Woodman's body?

c. Who had made the Tin Woodman in the first place?

d. Where were the Scarecrow's clothes?

e. How did the Tin Woodman help them get the clothes?

f. What did the Winkies stuff the Scarecrow with?

7. Here are some events from Chapter 20:
   * Dorothy freed the Lion.
   * The Witch made an iron bar invisible.
   * Dorothy threw a bucket of water at the Witch.
   * The Witch melted away.
   a. Write the event that occurred **first**.
   b. Write the event that occurred **next**.
   c. Write the event that occurred **last**.

PART C   Review Items

8. **Use the words in the box to fill in the blanks or replace the underlined words.**

presence	slightest	requested
admit	advanced	weep
permit	preferred	scent
meek	scatter	pure
	tremendous	

   a. The smoke had a very strange <u>smell</u>.

b. Ron went to work, but he <u>would have chosen</u> to sleep.

c. The king was bored and welcomed the clown's _____ .

d. When you are very sad you sometimes <u>cry</u> loudly.

e. Something <u>that's very big</u> is _____ .

f. The <u>smallest</u> noise would wake him.

g. The water was as clear and _____ as any they had tasted.

h. The ants seemed to move slowly, but they <u>moved forward</u> more than ten miles in a day.

i. When Martha tossed the seeds, she tried to _____ them evenly.

j. Jan <u>asked for</u> a salad and a glass of milk.

PART D   Writing Assignment

Why do you think the water melted the Witch? Write a paragraph that explains your answer. Be sure the paragraph answers the following questions:
   * What kind of person was the Witch?
   * Why was the water more powerful than the Witch?

Make your paragraph at least **four** sentences long.

Lesson 26

PART A   Word Lists

1	2	3
reunited	handsome	**Vocabulary words**
bracelet	costume	1. reunited
tongue	husband	2. bracelet
mischief	guest	3. inlaid
ache	prompt	4. grumble
	promptly	5. plead
		6. exclaim
		7. promptly

PART B   Story Items

1. Why did the travelers decide to go back to the Emerald City?
2. Write which traveler received each gift from the Winkies.
   a. A silver oilcan
   b. A gold-headed walking stick
   c. A beautiful diamond bracelet
   d. A golden collar
3. Dorothy found the golden cap in the Witch's cupboard.
   a. Who could Dorothy command with the golden cap?
   b. Did Dorothy know about the power of the golden cap?
   c. Why did Dorothy take the golden cap?
4. a. The Witch that ruled the Winkies lived in the Land of the _____.
   b. Dorothy and the others wanted to go from that land to the Emerald City. Name the direction they would have to go.
   c. They knew they would have to go toward
      ● the stars.   ● the Winkies.
      ● the setting sun.   ● the rising sun.
5. The travelers got lost when the sun was not in the east and not in the west. What time of day was that?
6. The next morning, the travelers started walking again. Why was it hard for them to know which direction was east?
7. a. What color were the fields?
   b. So the travelers knew they were still in the Land of the _____.
   c. Name **two** flowers the travelers saw in the fields.
8. At the end of the chapter, Dorothy felt
   ● happy.   ● amazed.
   ● discouraged. ● rested.

PART C   Review Items

9. Write which character could have said each sentence.
   a. "The Winkies gave me a diamond bracelet."
   b. "The Witch kept me in her courtyard."
   c. "I am happy that my dents were fixed."
   d. "There is no place like home."
   e. "I really like my new straw."
   f. "The Winkies gave me a silver oilcan."
   g. "The Monkeys threw my clothes into a tree."
   h. "I am supposed to be the King of Beasts."
   i. "The Winkies gave me a walking stick."
   j. "I think I'll try on this golden cap."

10. **Use the words in the box to fill in the blanks or replace the underlined words.**

resolved	requested	pack
admit	great anger	husky
terror	marble	huge
swarm	flock	strike

   a. The plate of roast beef was so <u>enormous</u> that Rosa could not eat it all.
   b. Julie ran away screaming in <u>great fear</u>.
   c. The sheep were in a _____.
   d. When the students became noisy the teacher <u>asked for</u> silence.
   e. The dogs moved in a large _____.
   f. The man held the hammer ready to <u>hit</u> the nail.
   g. The bees flew in a thick _____.
   h. When John heard the terrible news, he felt <u>rage</u>.

PART D   Writing Assignment

The travelers are lost. Write a story that tells how the travelers finally get back to the Emerald City. Be sure the paragraph answers the following questions:
● How did the travelers find their way?
● What happened on their journey back to the Emerald City?

Lesson 27

PART A   Word Lists

1
Gayla
Quel
ventriloquist
uneasily
bulged

2
promptly
fortunately
solemnly
presently

3
Vocabulary words
1. pattering
2. mischief
3. lining
4. spare
5. bride
6. capture

PART B   Story Items

1. The travelers had met the field mice before.
   a. Who had saved the Queen from a wildcat?
   b. Who had the field mice saved?
2. Dorothy called someone who could tell the travelers how to get to the Emerald City.
   a. Who did Dorothy call?
   b. That person told Dorothy to call _____.
   c. What object did Dorothy use to call them?
   d. Where were the instructions for calling the Monkeys?
   e. What did Dorothy command the Monkeys to do?
3. At first, the Scarecrow and the Tin Woodman were frightened of the Monkeys.
   a. What had the Monkeys done to the Scarecrow?
   b. What had the Monkeys done to the Tin Woodman?
4. The King Monkey told Dorothy what the Monkeys were like before they had to obey the owner of the golden cap.
   a. At that time, the Monkeys lived in the Land of the _____.
   b. At that time, did the Monkeys have to obey anyone?
   c. When the monkeys were free, they were
      • slaves.   • sad.
      • full of mischief.   • serious.

5. a. Gayla decided to marry _____.
   b. What did the Monkeys do to Quel?
   c. What happened to Quel's fine clothes?
6. Gayla finally decided to spare the Monkeys.
   a. The Monkeys agreed to obey the person who owned the _____.
   b. The person who had that object could command the Monkeys _____ times.
   c. Who was the first owner of the golden cap?
7. The golden cap fell into the hands of an evil character.
   a. Who was that character?
   b. Name the last things the Monkeys did for that character.

PART C   Review Items

8. Write whether each statement describes the **Munchkins,** the **Kalidahs,** the **Winkies,** or the **Winged Monkeys.**
   a. They had to obey whoever owned the golden cap.
   b. They wore blue hats.
   c. They wore yellow clothes.
   d. They liked to make mischief.
   e. They had heads like tigers and bodies like bears.
   f. They threw Quel into a river.
   g. They had farms in the Land of the East.

9. Use the words in the box to fill in the blanks or replace the underlined words.

requested	acted very happy
comforted	desperately
seized	cunning
singed	studded
meek	tempt
rage	terror

a. Victor deserved more money, but he was too timid to ask for it.

b. Jan asked for a salad and a glass of milk.

c. The paper was black after being slightly burned in the fire.

d. The policemen grabbed the crook.

e. Max held the meat near the fence and tried to _____ the dog.

f. When the rock hit the hive, the bees responded with great anger.

g. The anxious traveler _____ wanted to catch the train.

h. Many thieves are very clever but sneaky.

i. When the work was over all the people rejoiced.

PART D   Writing Assignment

What would you do if you had wings and could fly wherever you wanted? Write a paragraph that explains your answer. Be sure the paragraph answers the following questions:
- Where would you live?
- How would you spend your time?

Make your paragraph at least **four** sentences long.

Lesson 28

PART A   Word Lists

1	2	3	4
uneasily	tongue	**Vocabulary words**	**Vocabulary words**
solemnly	ventriloquism	1. plead	1. tiresome
presently	ache	2. exclaim	2. bald
fortunately	ached	3. promptly	3. overheard
promptly	balloonist		4. humbug
	liquid		5. ventriloquist
	bulge		6. imitate
	bulged		7. confidence
			8. consider
			9. gradually
			10. uneasy

PART B Story Items

1. a. How did the Guardian of the Gates feel when he saw the travelers?
   b. Why did the Guardian bow to Dorothy?
2. At first, Oz would not see the travelers. What did the Scarecrow threaten to do?
3. Oz was frightened because he had met the Winged Monkeys before. What had they done at that time?
4. a. What did the travelers see when they entered the throne room?
   b. What did the travelers hear when they entered the throne room?
5. Toto knocked over the screen.
   a. What kind of person was standing behind the screen?
   b. Was Oz a wizard or a humbug?
6. Oz explained how he had fooled the travelers.
   a. What material was the great head made of?
   b. Why could Oz make the head talk?
   c. What did Oz wear to look like a lovely lady?
   d. What was the beast made out of?
   e. What was the ball of fire made of?
7. Here are some events from Chapter 23:
   • Toto knocked over a screen.
   • The Scarecrow threatened to call the Winged Monkeys.
   • The Guardian of the Gates met the travelers.
   a. Write the event that occurred **first.**
   b. Write the event that occurred **next.**
   c. Write the event that occurred **last.**

PART C Review Items

8. Write the **color** of things in each place.
   a. Emerald City
   b. Land of the Winkies
   c. Land of the Munchkins

9. Write whether each event happened in the **forest,** the **throne room,** or the **witch's castle.**
   a. The Lion saw a ball of fire.
   b. Dorothy threw a bucket of water at somebody.
   c. The Kalidahs attacked the travelers.
   d. Dorothy found a cap in a cupboard.
   e. Oz gave Dorothy a command.
10. **Use the words in the box to fill in the blanks or replace the underlined words.**

great fear	cruelty	tint
advanced	tenderly	huge
desperately	admit	weep

   a. When he saw the bear he gasped in terror.
   b. Dorothy and the others moved forward toward the marvelous city.
   c. The guardian would not _____ her to the marvelous city.
   d. She wanted to do well, so she _____ tried to succeed.
   e. The witch laughed with _____.
   f. She held her dog gently and lovingly.

PART D Writing Assignment

Write a paragraph that explains how Oz made Dorothy believe he was a giant head. Be sure the paragraph answers the following questions:
• What was the head made out of?
• How did the head move?
• How did the head speak?

Make your paragraph at least **four** sentences long.

Lesson 29

PART A Word Lists

1	2	3
experience	imagination	**Vocabulary words**
knowledge	hesitation	1. high spirits
congratulate	explanation	2. knowledge
deceive	imitation	3. experience
imitate		4. congratulate
		5. contents
		6. deceive

PART B Story Items

1. **a.** Where was Oz born?
   b. First, Oz was trained by a great master to be a
   - balloonist.
   - humbug.
   - wizard.
   - ventriloquist.
   c. Next, he became a
   - ventriloquist.
   - balloonist.
   - humbug.
   - wizard.
   d. Which job did he have when he worked for a circus?

2. One day, Oz was carried away in his balloon.
   a. The balloon carried Oz to _____.
   b. When people first saw him, they thought he was a _____.
   c. What did Oz order the people to build?

3. Oz ordered all the people to wear green spectacles.
   a. Was the Emerald City really green?
   b. Why do most of the people think the Emerald City is green?

4. Oz was afraid of the Wicked Witches.
   a. Did Oz have any magic powers?
   b. Did the Witches have any magic powers?
   c. What would the Witches have done to Oz if they had known the truth?
   d. Who finally destroyed the Wicked Witches?

5. Oz told the Lion that what he really needed was
   - pins and needles.
   - courage.
   - a heart.
   - confidence.

6. Oz told the Tin Woodman that a heart made people feel a certain way. Oz thinks a heart makes people feel
   - unhappy.
   - happy.
   - frightened.
   - amazed.

7. The Scarecrow went to see Oz the next day.
   a. Name **two** things that Oz put inside the Scarecrow's head.
   b. Oz told the Scarecrow that those two things showed that he was
   - brave.
   - courageous.
   - sharp.
   - happy.

PART C Review Items

8. **Use the words in the box to fill in the blanks or replace the underlined words.**

deserted	tempt	large meal
reunited	rage	pleaded with
scatter	advanced	strike
cunning	on time	mend
huge	inlaid	

   a. Walt could never find shoes big enough to fit his _____ feet.
   b. After staying in the same place for a week, the armies _____ five more miles.
   c. The Witch shouted with <u>great anger</u> at Dorothy.
   d. The splendid things he promised her did not _____ her.

e. The Witch was very cruel and <u>clever</u> but <u>sneaky</u>.
f. He sat down at the table and prepared to have a <u>feast</u>.
g. He was ready to throw his shirt away, but she said that she could <u>fix</u> it.
h. The friends <u>rejoiced</u> when they were <u>together again</u> at last.
i. <u>Kim's</u> ring was ——————— with expensive jewels.
j. She <u>begged</u> the witch to let her go.
k. When the clock rings, get up <u>promptly</u>.

PART D   Writing Assignment

Do you think the Scarecrow will be different now that he has brains? Write a paragraph that explains your answer. Be sure the paragraph answers the following questions:
- How did the Scarecrow act before he had brains?
- How will the Scarecrow act now that he has brains?

Make your paragraph at least **four** sentences long.

Lesson 30

PART A   Word Lists

1
congratulation
hesitation
imitation
explanation
imagination

2
Vocabulary words
1. imitate
2. confidence
3. consider
4. uneasy
5. contents
6. deceive
7. gradually

3
Vocabulary words
1. shears
2. sawdust
3. replaced
4. tug

PART B   Story Items

1. The Woodman went to see Oz.
   a. What did Oz do with the shears?
   b. What did Oz put in the Tin Woodman's chest?
   c. What was the heart made out of?
2. The Lion went to see Oz.
   a. Oz told the Lion the liquid in the dish was ———————.
   b. Did the Lion want to drink the liquid at first?
   c. Why did the Lion have to drink all the liquid?
3. Oz decided to take Dorothy back to Kansas in a balloon.
   a. What was the balloon made out of?
   b. What color was the balloon?
4. a. If the air inside a balloon is hot, the balloon will ———————.
   b. If the air inside a balloon gets cold, the balloon will ———————.
   c. What did Oz fill the balloon with?
5. a. Where did the air come from?
   b. What did Oz tie to the bottom of the balloon?
      - Toto
      - a clothes basket
      - hot air
      - rocks
6. Oz was ready to leave.
   a. What held the balloon to the ground?
   b. Why did Dorothy go into the crowd?
   c. What happened to the ropes?
   d. What happened to the balloon?

7. **a.** Did the people ever see Oz again?
   b. How did the people of the Emerald City feel after Oz left?
8. **a.** What character chased a kitten into the crowd?
   b. Who followed that character?
   c. Who was left in the basket?

PART C   Review Items

9. **Use the words in the box to fill in the blanks or replace the underlined words.**

tremendous	hit	flock
capturing	tint	swarm
mischief	oats	begged
cruelty	pack	timid
cunning	fix	inlaid

   a. Most wild animals are very <u>meek</u> and will run away from humans.
   b. To move the huge safe, they had to give it a <u>great</u> push.
   c. The dogs moved in a large group.
   d. If you miss that nail you will <u>strike</u> your finger.

   e. She knew he was lying but he was so _____ that she could not prove it.
   f. The bees flew in a thick <u>group</u>.
   g. The Wicked Witch acted with _____ when she wouldn't feed the Lion.
   h. The sheep were in a <u>group</u>.
   i. The sock had so many holes in it, nobody could <u>mend</u> it.
   j. They <u>pleaded</u> for another chance.
   k. The Winged Monkeys were always getting into some kind of _____.
   l. Indians were very skillful at <u>catching</u> horses.

PART D   Writing Assignment

Write a story that tells what happened to Oz after he left the Emerald City. Be sure the story answers the following questions:
• Where did the balloon take him?
• What happened to him when the balloon landed?

Lesson 31

PART A   Word Lists

1
towel
vibrate
underneath
collar

2
precious
ventriloquism
thorough
through

3
Vocabulary words
1. whisk
2. farewell
3. extend
4. dose
5. utter
6. hush

PART B
Reading Checkout Rules

1. If I read the passage in less than one minute, I get points as follows:
   No errors—3 points.
   1 or 2 errors—1 point.
   More than 2 errors—no points.
2. If I take more than one minute to read the passage, I get no points. But I will reread the passage until I can read it in one minute with no more than 2 errors.
3. I will write the number of points I earn in the checkout box for today's lesson.

PART C   Story Items

1. **a.** Who left in the balloon?
   b. Did Dorothy know how to get back to Kansas without that person?
2. At the beginning of the chapter, Dorothy wiped away the Tin Woodman's tears.
   a. What would have happened to the Tin Woodman if Dorothy had not wiped the tears away?
   b. What did the Tin Woodman put on his joints after he cried?
3. The travelers met in the throne room.
   a. Which character was sitting on the throne?
   b. Why was that character sitting there?
   c. Name the three characters that were content.
   d. Name the character that was not content.
   e. Why was that character not content?
4. One character might know a way to cross the desert.
   a. What is that character's name?
   b. In which land does that character live?
   c. Who carried Dorothy to that land?

PART D   Review Items

5. Write whether each sentence describes the **Witch of the East,** the **Witch of the North,** or the **Witch of the West.**
   a. This Witch made the Winkies her slaves.
   b. This Witch lived with the Gillikins.
   c. This Witch was killed by Dorothy's house.
   d. This Witch told the wolves to kill the travelers.
   e. This Witch gave Dorothy a kiss.
   f. This Witch had owned the golden cap.
   g. This Witch made the Munchkins her slaves.

6. Use the words in the box to fill in the blanks or replace the underlined words.

slightest	bride
rejoiced	inlaid
gently and lovingly	feast
desperately	pure
preferred	on time
together again	spare
battered	

   a. The girl ate apples, but she _____ peaches.
   b. As Sheila climbed the cliff, she _____ held onto the rope.
   c. Everybody _____ and had a marvelous celebration.
   d. They were very full after their Thanksgiving _____.
   e. Sam had to handle the roses <u>tenderly</u> or they would fall apart.
   f. Most of the time she came here <u>promptly</u>, but sometimes, she was <u>late</u>.
   g. The jewels in the crown were _____ in delightful patterns.
   h. After being separated for many years, the brothers were <u>reunited</u>.
   i. The hunter will _____ the deer and let it go free.
   j. Maria was twenty years old when she became his _____.

PART E   Writing Assignment

Where would you rather live, at home or in the Emerald City? Write a paragraph that explains your answer. Be sure the paragraph answers the following questions:
- How is the Emerald City better than your home?
- How is your home better than the Emerald City?

Make your paragraph at least **four** sentences long.

Lesson 32

PART A   Word Lists

1	2	3
ease	overheard	**Vocabulary words**
chorus	singe	1. disgusting
echo	grant	2. chorus
	crackling	
	giant	
	cackling	
	timid	
	timidly	

PART B   Story Items

1. The travelers came to a farmhouse. What color was the house?
2. The travelers saw Glinda.
   a. What was Glinda's throne made out of?
   b. What color was her hair?
   c. What color was her dress?
3. Dorothy told Glinda that she wanted to go back to Kansas.
   a. What did Glinda ask Dorothy to give her?
   b. Where will the Scarecrow go after Dorothy leaves?
   c. What will he do there?
   d. Where will the Tin Woodman go after Dorothy leaves?
   e. What will he do there?
   f. Where will the Lion go after Dorothy leaves?
   g. What will he do there?
4. What **two** things did Dorothy have to do to make the shoes work?
5. a. What was the last thing that Dorothy said at the end of the story?
   b. What color was everything near the Emerald City?
   c. What color was everything in the Land of the Munchkins?
   d. What color was everything in the Land of the Winkies?
   e. What color was everything in the Land of the Quadlings?

PART C   Review Items

6. Write whether each sentence describes the **Munchkins,** the **Winkies,** or the **Winged Monkeys.**
   a. They wore blue hats with bells on them.
   b. They had to obey whoever owned the golden cap.
   c. They could fly in the air.
   d. They gave the travelers many gifts.
   e. They slaved for the Witch of the East.
   f. They wore yellow clothes.
7. **Use the words in the box to fill in the blanks or replace the underlined words.**

acted very happy	spare
congratulated	pleaded with
ventriloquist	strike
desperately	imitate
considered	mischief
experience	tint
confidence	deceived
tenderly	gradual

a. When they put the lion in a cage, it tried _____ to get out.

b. When the team won the game, everybody _____ .

c. Stan begged her not to enter the terrible forest.

d. Those little puppies were full of _____ when they tore up the garden.

e. Gardeners don't _____ weeds, they kill every one.

f. Janet was not a very good _____ because her mouth always moved.

g. Martin could _____ the strange way the ducks walked.

h. Kelly had _____ in the players on the team.

i. The jeweler offered her a lot of money, and she _____ the offer.

j. The change was not sudden but was very _____ .

k. Sitting through the horror movie was a frightening _____ .

l. They _____ him for his fine speech.

m. Although Juan felt sad, he wore a smile that _____ people.

PART D   Writing Assignment

Do you think that the Land of Oz is a real place? Write a paragraph that explains your answer. Be sure the paragraph answers the following questions:

- In what ways is the Land of Oz real?
- In what ways is the Land of Oz not real?

Make your paragraph at least **four** sentences long.

Lesson 33

PART A   Word Lists

1	2	3
snarling	**Vocabulary words**	**Vocabulary words**
worry	1. extend	1. reeds
braid	2. chorus	2. ease
worries	3. hush	3. echo
fierce	4. utter	4. bruise
duckling	5. disgusting	
valley		
blossom		
swan		

PART B   Hyphens

Sometimes, words that appear at the end of a printed line are too long to fit on that line. So only the first part of the word appears on the line. That part is followed by a hyphen, which is a mark that looks like this: -Ⓐ

The rest of the word appears at the beginning of the next line.

The next column has a passage with words that run from the end of one line to the beginning of the next line.Ⓑ

That morning Dorothy kissed the pretty green girl goodbye. Then the four travelers walked through the Emerald City toward the gate. When the guard saw them approaching, he knew that they were planning to go on a new adventure. As he unlocked their green spectacles, he congratulated the Scarecrow, who was now the ruler of the city. The guard smiled and gladly shook the Scarecrow's hand.

PART C   Story Items

1. **a.** How many eggs were in the mother duck's nest?
   b. What color were five of the eggs?
   c. What color was the other egg?
   d. What would have happened to the ducklings if the mother duck did not stay on the eggs?
2. **a.** How many times had the mother duck laid eggs before those eggs?
   b. Why did the mother duck examine the eggs several times a day?
3. **a.** What hatched first, the five eggs or the other egg?
   b. What came out of the five eggs?
   c. What did a neighbor duck think the strange egg might be?

   The other ducks dislike the ugly duckling just because he is different. Do you think that people might also dislike someone who is different? Write a paragraph that explains your answer.

   Make your paragraph at least **four** sentences long.

4. **a.** What color was the last duckling that hatched?
      - brown   • yellow   • white
   b. Name two other ways that the duckling was different from the others.
   c. How did the other adult ducks treat that duckling?
5. At last the duckling became so sad that it decided to do something.
   a. What was that?
   b. What were the other ducks doing when the duckling carried out its plan?
6. Write which character could have made each statement. Choose from the **ugly duckling,** the **mother duck,** or the **mean duck.**
   a. "This large egg is a lot of trouble."
   b. "He may not be handsome, but he is strong."
   c. "I don't fit in."
   d. "I would rather run away than stay here."
   e. "I'll snap at that duckling when the mother isn't looking."
   f. "I cannot expect all of my children to be beautiful."
   g. "I am tired of being picked on."
   h. "That ugly duck is a disgrace."

PART D   Review Items

7. **Use the words in the box to fill in the blanks or replace the underlined words.**

gradually	mend
confidence	pack
ventriloquist	flock
caught	swarm
promptly	terror
tenderly	replace
trick	admit
bride	

   a. Paula smiled at the baby and played gently and lovingly with it.
   b. Someone who is never late always arrives on time.
   c. They captured the Tin Woodman and threw him into a dark room.
   d. The bees flew in a thick

   _____.
   e. A _____ can make it seem like someone else is doing the talking.
   f. When she slipped, she began to lose her _____.
   g. The wolves moved in a large

   _____.

h. The colors began to change _____.

i. The Witch tried to <u>deceive</u> the Scarecrow but she did not succeed.

j. The birds were in a _____.

k. Her mother told her to _____ the glass that she had used.

l. The _____ looked pretty in her white gown.

Lesson 34

PART A — Word Lists

1
blow
scratch
strangle
bowl
stretch
struggle

2
Vocabulary words
1. reflection
2. moss

PART B — Hyphens

What is the name for this mark: – ?(A)

Read the hyphenated words in the passage below.(B)

The sun was bright as the friends slowly turned toward the Land of the Quadlings. They were all cheerful and chatted happily. Dorothy was now almost certain that she would get home, and the Woodman smiled at her. The brave Lion was wagging his tail back and forth. He was joyful to be outside again. Toto was chasing butterflies, jumping around, and barking merrily all the time.

PART E — Writing Assignment

The other ducks dislike the ugly duckling just because he is different. Do you think that people might also dislike someone who is different? Write a paragraph that explains your answer.

Make your paragraph at least **four** sentences long.

PART C — Story Items

1. a. The duckling first wandered into a group of _____.

b. Did those birds care that the duckling was ugly?

c. Why did the duckling want to stay with the geese forever?

2. Two young geese asked the duckling to leave the plain with them.

a. What happened to those two geese?

b. Why didn't the duckling fly away with the other geese?

3. Why did the duckling think that the dog did not eat him?

4. One day, the duckling saw a flock of swans flying by.

a. What color were the swans?

b. In which direction were the swans flying?

c. Why were they flying in that direction?

d. Did the duckling want to go with them?

e. Why did the duckling think that he wouldn't be a good companion for the swans?

5. One day, the duckling almost froze to death.

a. Who rescued the duckling?

b. Who wanted to play with the duckling?

6. The duckling saw something pink on the side of a hill.

a. What time of year was it?

b. How did the duckling get to the pink thing?

c. Had he ever done that before?

d. What was the pink thing?

7. The duckling saw a group of swans on the river.

a. What did the swans do as the duckling approached?

b. How did the duckling discover how he looked?

c. What did the duckling look like now?

d. Who saw the duckling spreading its wings?

e. What did that animal think of the duckling now?

PART D   Review Items

8. Use the words in the box to fill in the blanks or replace the underlined words.

congratulated	mischief
experience	cruelty
confidence	plead
replacing	goodbye
extended	tricking
cunning	

    a. The children could not be left alone because they would get into

    _____.

    b. Eric was not afraid to walk the tight rope because he had _____ in his ability.

    c. Not one person _____ Dan for winning the race.

    d. She had an exciting _____ at the beach.

    e. When they lied, he knew they were <u>deceiving</u> him.

    f. They had a hard time _____ all the things that had been stolen.

    g. Beth said <u>farewell</u> to all of the friends she was leaving.

    h. She _____ her arms out as far as she could reach.

PART E   Writing Assignment

Write a short story that is like "The Ugly Duckling" except make the main character a boy or a girl. Explain how the boy or girl feels about being ugly. Then explain what happens in the end.

Lesson 35

PART A   Hyphens

What is the name for this mark? –Ⓐ
Read the hyphenated words in the passage below.Ⓑ

    In the morning they tra-veled until they reached a for-est. There was no way of go-ing around it. It seemed to ex-tend to the right and left far-ther than they could see. How-ever, the Woodman and the Scare-crow left the group and soon dis-covered a way to enter the for-est.

PART B   Review Items

1. **Use the words in the box to fill in the blanks or replace the underlined words.**

tiny green plants	rage
congratulated	group
disgusting	spare
experience	utter
mischief	capture
considered	contents
imitate	reflection

a. She used a large net to <u>catch</u> butterflies.

b. He _____ reading the book, but it looked boring.

c. The <u>things inside</u> of the large trunk had <u>disappeared.</u>

d. If you have never done it before, it is a new _____.

e. They all _____ her when she won the spelling contest.

f. Those little puppies were full of _____ when they got into the clothes basket.

g. Some of Dorothy's experiences were horrible and _____.

h. She did not <u>say</u> a sound.

i. The rocks were green because they were covered with <u>moss</u>.

j. The actor admired his _____ in the mirror.

PART C   Writing Assignment

Write a poem about a place that you like. Describe how the place looks and explain why you like the place. Your poem does not have to rhyme.

Lesson 36

PART A   Word Lists

1	2	3
England	sway	**Vocabulary words**
London	disbelief	1. barbed wire
Derick	inexpensive	2. alert
ridiculous	swayed	3. nag
		4. pasture
		5. strand
		6. develops
		7. plod
		8. thoroughbred
		9. nudge

PART B   Story Items

1. a. What time of day was it when Tara first saw how Nellie got out of the pasture?
   b. What lit up the sky so that Tara could see her clearly?
2. Tara found two things amazing about Nellie.
   a. She looked so _____.
   b. She could _____.
3. Later, when Nellie jumped the fence, Tara found her in a _____.
4. Tara told her father about a plan for keeping Nellie in the pasture.
   a. What was that plan?
   b. Why didn't her father approve of the plan?
5. Why didn't the plan of tying Nellie in the barn work very well?

PART C   Review Items

6. Write whether each statement about Oz is **true** or **false.**
   a. He was a ball of fire.
   b. He made a fake heart for the Tin Woodman.
   c. He left the Land of Oz forever.
   d. He was a ventriloquist.
   e. He built a balloon.
   f. He put pins and needles in the Scarecrow's head.
   g. He had magic powers.
   h. He was more powerful than the Witches.
   i. He ordered people to wear glasses.
   j. He could take any form he wanted.

7. Use the words in the box to fill in the blanks or replace the underlined words.

things that were inside	extended
confidence	utter
disgusting	caught
replaced	echo
bruised	dose
cunning	chorus
	slowly

a. Mountain goats walk with _____ and never worry about falling.
b. They thought they would never get across the sea, but <u>gradually</u> they got closer to the other side.
c. Sharon spilled the <u>contents</u> of the bottle all over the floor.
d. The policeman <u>captured</u> many crooks.
e. For a while it was missing, but somebody finally _____ it.
f. The road <u>stretched out</u> all the way across the plain.
g. The food was too <u>horrible</u> to eat.
h. Martha felt better after taking her _____ of medicine.
i. When Harumi shouted she heard her _____.
j. Her legs were _____ after she fell.

PART D   Writing Assignment

Mr. Briggs wants to get rid of Nellie. Perhaps Nellie could be trained not to jump.

Write **four** sentences that tell how you would train her.

Lesson 37

PART A Word Lists

1	2	3	4
encyclopedia	mound	**Vocabulary words**	**Vocabulary words**
steeplechase	loudly	1. nudge	1. resist the impulse
obstacles	ground	2. alert	2. barrier and obstacle
exhaustion	mounted	3. develop	3. cock your head
endurance	sound		4. blurt out
	grouch		5. stall
			6. stray
			7. exhausted
			8. endurance

PART B Story Items

1. What problem did the Briggs have with Nellie?
2. At night Tara thought of a plan for solving that problem. What was her plan?
3. Tara had to get facts about training Nellie.
   a. What was the first thing she did to try to find out some facts?
   b. Where did she find a lot of facts about steeplechases?
4. a. Write **two** ways a steeplechase is different from a regular horse race.
   b. Write **three** types of barriers that horses must go over in a steeplechase.
   c. Which kind of jump is the most dangerous?
   d. What is the only requirement for horses to enter a steeplechase?
5. a. Tara started looking through books just before _____.
   b. Who came down the stairs and gave Tara a suggestion about how to get more facts?
   c. That person suggested that Tara should talk to _____.
6. What did Tara hear as she approached the village?
7. a. What kind of shop did Mr. Jones operate?
   b. What did Mr. Jones say he would do if Nellie could really jump?
   c. What did Nellie do to prove that she could jump really well?

PART C Review Items

8. a. Write the name of the gem that is red.
   b. Write the name of the gem that is clear.
   c. Write the name of the gem that is green.
   d. What's another name for a whirlwind or a twister?
9. **Use the words in the box to fill in the blanks or replace the underlined words.**

congratulated	contents
bruise	echo
extend	moss
considered	said

   a. They _____ not going to the party at all.
   b. The teacher _____ Mike for being such a good reader.
   c. They opened the can and ate the things that were inside.
   d. Slowly, they uttered the pledge.
   e. Manuel's _____ repeated everything he said.
   f. The _____ on his arm hurt.

PART D Writing Assignment

Write at least **four** sentences that tell why you think Nellie would be a very good steeplechase horse.

Lesson 38

PART A Word Lists

1
anvil
Arabian
abruptly
Ealing
dilapidated

2
demonstrate
select
encyclopedia
customer
mayor
competition
thirty

3
Vocabulary words
1. blurt out
2. resist the impulse
3. barrier and obstacle
4. endurance
5. exhausted

4
Vocabulary words
1. brace yourself
2. abruptly
3. gallop
4. dilapidated
5. marvel
6. spectators
7. mock

PART B Story Items

1. **a.** What had Mr. Jones said that he would do if Nellie proved that she could jump well?
   b. How did Nellie demonstrate that she could jump well?
2. Mr. Jones set up a course for training Tara and Nellie.
   a. Where was that course?
   b. How many jumps were in that course?
   c. How high were the jumps at first?
3. Mr. Jones said that he would raise the jumps when something happened.
   a. What was that?
   b. How long did the jumps stay at the same height before they were raised?
4. Complete the following sentences.
   a. At first, Tara fell off Nellie when she was _____.
   • taking off   • landing
   b. Later, Tara fell off Nellie when she was _____.
   • taking off   • landing
   c. Tara fell off _____ when Nellie was taking off.
   • backwards   • forwards
   d. Tara fell off _____ when Nellie was landing.
   • backwards   • forwards
5. How wide was the streambed at the place where Nellie practiced?

6. **a.** When Tara and Mr. Jones returned to the blacksmith shop, who was waiting for them?
   b. That person was angry because Mr. Jones hadn't _____ .
   c. What did Mr. Jones say he would do if Nellie did not win the jumping contest at Ealing?

PART C Review Items

7. **a.** What color was everything near the Emerald City?
   b. What color was everything in the Land of the Munchkins?
   c. What color was everything in the Land of the Winkies?
   d. What color was everything in the Land of the Quadlings?
8. **Use the words in the box to fill in the blanks or replace the underlined words.**

plodding	alert
resisted the impulse	singed
gradually	echo
knowledge	uttered
deceived	grew
endurance	capture
experiences	pasture
extended	

a. They advanced so <u>slowly</u> that you could barely see that <u>they were</u> moving.
b. The clever movements of the fox <u>tricked</u> the hunter, and the fox escaped.
c. Someone who had lived a long time has had many _____ .
d. If you know a lot, you have a great deal of _____ .
e. Bob <u>stretched out</u> the rubber band until it snapped.
f. At last Kent <u>said</u> a word.
g. The rosebud <u>developed</u> into a flower.
h. The mother wolf stayed <u>full of attention</u> and did not sleep.
i. The horse ran across the <u>field for farm animals</u>.
j. The tired horses were <u>moving at a very slow, tired pace</u> <u>up the hill</u>.
k. She can keep on running because she has a great deal of _____ .
l. The child _____ to buy a new game.

PART D Writing Assignment

Pretend that you are riding Nellie when she jumps all the way across the stream.

Write at least **five** sentences that describe what happens and how you feel.

Lesson 39

PART A Word Lists

1	2	3	4
official	decorate	**Vocabulary words**	**Vocabulary words**
circular	Arabian	1. brace yourself	1. mount a horse
triangular	fiftieth	2. mock	2. officials
Rudy	hooves	3. abruptly	3. shabby
reins		4. gallop	4. numb
numb		5. dilapidated	
		6. marvel	
		7. spectators	

PART B   Story Items

1. About how many spectators were at the race?
2. a. Which two jumps were the most difficult in the course at Ealing?
   b. Why were those jumps particularly difficult?
3. a. What happened to Tara when the race began?
   b. What was she holding to prevent Nellie from running away?
4. Is a rider out of the race if the rider falls?
5. When Nellie was clearing the first jump, where were the other horses?
6. a. Did Tara let Nellie run at full speed?
   b. Tell why.
7. a. What color was the most beautiful horse?
   b. What color was Nellie?
8. a. What kind of jump did Nellie and the mayor's horse approach at the same time?
   b. What did Nellie do at that jump?
   c. What did the mayor's horse do?
9. a. Which horse was leading the competition at the end of the story?
   b. How much ground had Nellie gained on that horse?
   c. How many jumps ahead of Nellie was that horse?

PART C   Review Items

10. Use the words in the box to fill in the blanks or replace the underlined words.

resisted the impulse	bruised
stray	utter
grew	obstacle
endurance	nudged
extended	chorus
single strip	blurted out
dilapidated	
moved at a very slow, tired pace	

a. She _____ her arms out as far as she could reach.
b. At first Carl had a small plan, but later it developed into a large one.
c. Every strand of her hair was braided.
d. Cara impatiently waited as her dog plodded after her.
e. She gently pushed him, but he would not wake up.
f. He didn't run when he wanted to, so he _____ to run.
g. The dog wandered far from home and became a _____ dog.
h. The tree had fallen in the middle of the road and was an _____.
i. People who can run for miles have a lot of ability to keep going.
j. She suddenly said the answer.
k. The house was in bad shape.

PART D   Writing Assignment

Pretend that you are riding a handsome horse next to Nellie.

Write at least **four** sentences that tell how you feel before the race starts and how you feel as you watch Nellie.

Lesson 40

PART A   Word Lists

1	2	3
concentrate	familiar	**Vocabulary words**
photographer	camera	**1.** push a horse too hard
idiot	statue	**2.** let a horse out
Kelvin	Nighthawk	**3.** hold a horse in
caution		**4.** caution
Liverpool		**5.** magnificent
		6. turf

PART B   Story Items

1. **a.** As Tara was racing, somebody yelled instructions about what she should do. Who yelled?
   b. What did that character tell Tara to do?
2. **a.** Which horse was the first to cross the finish line?
   b. Why didn't that horse win the race?
   c. What had happened to the rider?
3. Why didn't Tara make Nellie run as fast as she could at the end of the race?
4. **a.** Who was waiting for Tara and the others at Mr. Jones' blacksmith shop?
   b. What did he want to buy?
   c. How much did he offer to pay?
   d. How many years would it take the Briggs family to earn that much money?
5. **a.** Which member of the Briggs family was thinking about selling Nellie?
   b. Which member of the Briggs family did not want to sell Nellie?
6. **a.** When Tara was back at the farm, who said that the Briggs family should not sell Nellie?
   b. That person said Nellie was worth more than _____ pounds.
7. **a.** Who were the two people standing in the doorway when Tara looked up?
   b. What did Tara's father say that made her start smiling again?

PART C   Review Items

8. **a.** Where did Dorothy see prairies?
   b. Where did Dorothy see blue fences?
   c. Where did Dorothy see walls studded with emeralds?
   d. Where did Dorothy see gray?
   e. What does a tinsmith do?
   f. What does a goldsmith do?
9. Here are some words that describe materials:
   - tough
   - soft
   - type of cotton
   - very fine
   a. Which words describe silk?
   b. Which word describes leather?
   c. Which word describes velvet?
   d. Which words describe gingham?

PART D   Writing Assignment

Mr. Briggs is thinking that he should sell Nellie.

Write at least **four** sentences that give reasons for selling Nellie.

Lesson 41

PART A   Word Lists

1	2	3	4	5
hedge	incredible	urge	**Vocabulary words**	**Vocabulary words**
sledge	photographer	eighteenth	1. turf	1. lagging behind
nudge	concentrate	twenty	2. caution	2. prance
ledge	microphone	twentieth	3. magnificent	3. dangling
	photograph			4. straining
				5. frantically

PART B   Story Items

1. Look at the picture of the course at Liverpool.

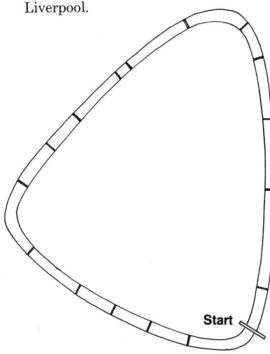

Start

   a. How long is the course at Liverpool?
   b. How many times do the horses go around the course?
   c. So how many miles do the horses run to finish the race?
   d. How many jumps are in the course the first time around?
   e. So how many jumps do the horses make to finish the race?
2. Nellie has just jumped the fifth jump on her second trip around the course.
   a. How many times has she jumped so far in the race?
   b. How many more times will she have to jump before she finishes the race?

3. a. The shape of the course at Liverpool is
   • rectangular.   • triangular.
   • circular.
   b. The shape of the course at Ealing is
   • rectangular.   • triangular.
   • circular.
4. Tara remembered what Mr. Longly had told her about the race at Liverpool.
   a. Mr. Longly didn't think that Nellie had enough _____ to win the Liverpool race.
   • endurance   • speed
   • age   • weight
   b. Which horse did Mr. Longly think would beat Nellie in the Liverpool race?
5. Before Nighthawk's rider fell off at Ealing, that rider was
   • holding Nighthawk in.
   • going full speed.
6. a. How many steeplechases had Nellie entered after winning the jumping contest at Ealing?
   b. How many had she won?
7. a. More than _____ horses entered the race at Liverpool.
   b. What was Nellie's number?
8. The announcer referred to two great horses that were in the race. The first was Nellie. The other horse was right next to Nellie. What was the name of that horse?
9. Write **two** things about the outfit that Tara wore at Liverpool that was different from the outfit she had worn at Ealing.
10. Write **two** reasons why the course at Liverpool was so demanding.

PART C   Review Items

11. Write whether each statement about Oz is **true** or **false**.
    a. He was a ball of fire.
    b. He made a fake heart for the Tin Woodman.
    c. He left the Land of Oz forever.
    d. He was a ventriloquist.
    e. He built a balloon.
    f. He put pins and needles in the Scarecrow's head.
    g. He had magic powers.
    h. He was more powerful than the witches.
    i. He ordered people to wear glasses.
    j. He could take any form he wanted.

12. **Use the words in the box to fill in the blanks or replace the underlined words.**

full of attention	numb
dilapidated	stray
gently pushing	spectators
endurance	officials
developed	shabby
braced himself	plod

    a. She was very poor and her clothes were in poor condition.

    b. When Pam started the race, nobody thought that she would have enough _____ to finish.
    c. The castle was very run down and in bad shape.
    d. The stands were filled with _____.
    e. Amanda had no feeling in her mouth, so her mouth was _____.
    f. The people who were responsible for everything being done right in the courtroom were the _____ of the courtroom.
    g. The young boy grew into a man.
    h. Franco knew that he was going to fall, so he tightened his muscles and got ready for a jolt.
    i. The child got her mother's attention by nudging her.

PART D   Writing Assignment

As the race of Liverpool begins, Tara thinks about many things.

Write at least **four** sentences that tell about some of the things she is thinking.

Lesson 42

PART A   Word Lists

1	2	3	4
advantage	continued	American Indians	couple
domestic	developed	garbage	civilized
relatives	returned	garage	uncivilized
examining	domesticated	alligators	receives
cooperation	required	humans	possible
unprotected			possibly

5
Vocabulary words
1. lagging behind
2. frantically
3. straining
4. dangling

6
Vocabulary words
1. domestic animals
2. relatives
3. jawbone
4. cooperate
5. venture
6. unprotected

PART B Story Items

1. Mr. Jones had told Tara to hold Nellie in until there were only _____ or _____ jumps left in the race.

2. Which horse matched Nellie stride for stride at the beginning of the race?

3. When they were going around the course the second time, Nighthawk did something that made Tara feel nervous. When that happened, Tara
   - held Nellie at an easy run.
   - pulled Nellie back.
   - let Nellie out.

4. When Nellie cleared the 26th jump, Tara
   - held Nellie at an easy run.
   - pulled Nellie back.
   - let Nellie out.

5. a. Who was ahead when Nellie cleared the 26th jump?
   b. About how far ahead?
   c. What did Nellie do after clearing that jump?

6. a. Which was the last jump that the horses went over together?
   b. Which horse landed ahead?
   c. Who won the race?

7. The announcer said that Nellie
   - tied a track record.
   - was close to the track record.
   - set a new track record.

8. a. How old was Nellie when she retired from steeplechase racing?
   b. By the time Nellie retired, she had won the Grand National Steeplechase Championship _____ times.

9. a. What does Tara have to remind her of Nellie?
   b. That horse won something that Nellie also won. What was that?

PART C Review Items

10. a. The main character in the Wizard of Oz was the person you read about from the beginning of the novel to the end. Who was the main character?
    b. There were **four** other characters that were almost as important. Name them.

11. a. Write the name of the gem that is green.
    b. Write the name of the gem that is red.
    c. Write the name of the gem that is clear.

12. When Dorothy came back to Kansas, it seemed to her that many things had a new color.
    a. What color had Kansas been before?
    b. Write the name of the place in Oz that the blue sky reminded her of.
    c. Write the name of the place that the yellow sun reminded her of.
    d. Write the name of the place that the green grass reminded her of.
    e. Write the name of the place that Aunt Em's red cheeks reminded her of.

13. **Use the words in the box to fill in the blanks or replace the underlined words.**

poorly made	mock
suddenly	stray
barriers	pasture
cautioned	numb
marvelous	strand

   a. The path was blocked with rocks, branches and other _____.
   b. A sheep wandered from the pasture and became a _____ sheep.
   c. Praise that is not sincere is _____ praise.
   d. When Marie awoke her legs felt cold and _____.
   e. Dorothy warned the Woodman about the danger.
   f. It was the most magnificent castle they had ever seen.
   g. She stopped very abruptly.

PART D Writing Assignment

In the story, Tara made a brief victory speech.

Write that speech. Make the speech at least **four** sentences long.

Lesson 43

PART A   Word Lists

1	2	3	4	5
successful	China	domestic	house cat	**Vocabulary words**
rodents	Africa	domesticate	half	1. advantages
prey	Asia	pieces	respect	2. rodents
guaranteed	Egypt	warmth	jerky	3. prey
generation	India	domesticated	keen	4. guarantee
		jawbone	eyesight	5. generation
		wolves		6. sleek
				7. keen

PART B   Story Items

1. All animals can be divided into two groups.
    a. Which group of animals does not live with people?
    b. Which group of animals lives with people?
2. For each of the following animals, write **wild** or **domestic.**
    a. tiger
    b. pig
    c. dog
    d. alligator
    e. chicken
    f. sheep
    g. lion
    h. bear
    i. cow
    j. horse
3. a. Which animal was the first to become domesticated?
    b. This animal was domesticated
        ● hundreds of years ago.
        ● thousands of years ago.
4. Which animal would be easier to domesticate, a wild puppy or a wild dog that is full-grown?
5. a. Name one reason wild dogs liked to live with people.
    b. Name one thing wild dogs could help people do.
6. Look at the picture of a garbage pile from an early cave.

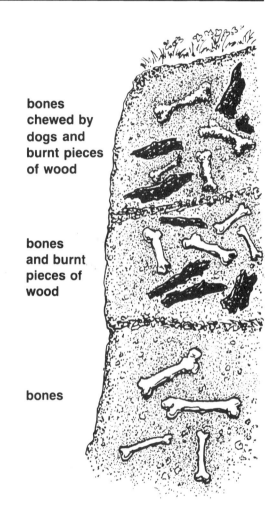

bones chewed by dogs and burnt pieces of wood

bones and burnt pieces of wood

bones

a. Which is closer to the bottom of the pile, burnt pieces of wood or bones?
b. So which went into the pile earlier, bones or burnt pieces of wood?
c. Which is closer to the bottom of the pile, burnt pieces of wood or bones chewed by dogs?
d. So which came first, the use of fire or the use of dogs?

7. People who lived in caves had to move from one place to another so they could
   - grow their own food.
   - find animals to hunt.
   - raise dogs.
8. Some people became farmers.
   a. Name one of the animals they domesticated.
   b. Did those people move from place to place?
   c. Who got more use out of animals—farmers or hunters?
   d. Name a product farmers got from goats.

PART C   Review Items

9. For each item, write **Briggs' Farm, Ealing,** or **Liverpool.**
   a. Where Nellie won her first race.
   b. Where the Grand National Steeplechase race was held.
   c. Where the race course is circular.
   d. Where Nellie lived.
   e. Where the race course is triangular.
10. **Use the words in the box to fill in the blanks or replace the underlined words.**

magnificent	warned
endurance	officials
developing	blurt out
straining	numb
lag behind	mock
ground covered with grass	

a. People who can run for miles have a lot of <u>ability to keep going</u>.
b. Her sympathy was not sincere. It was _____ sympathy.
c. There were five _____ at the steeplechase.
d. They said that her costume was the most <u>marvelous</u> one at the party.
e. The horse stumbled and tossed the rider to the <u>turf</u>.
f. Near the end of the race, the black horse began to <u>drop back</u>.
g. The horses were grunting and _____ while they were racing.
h. The sign <u>cautioned</u> them about using the bridge.

PART D   Writing Assignment

What do you think would have happened if people had never domesticated animals?

Write at least **four** sentences that explain your answer.

Lesson 44

1	2	3	4
popular	falcon	camel	generation
talons	hawk	mongoose	domestication
various	dove	cheetah	Egyptian
	turkey	donkey	position
		weasel	cooperation
		llama	
		mule	
		cobra	

5
Vocabulary words
1. advantages
2. unprotected
3. venture
4. cooperate
5. relatives

6
Vocabulary words
1. generation
2. guarantee
3. prey
4. rodents

PART B   Story Items

1. **a.** What was the first animal to be domesticated?
   b. What was that animal used for?
2. Name the use for each domesticated animal. Choose from **hunting, food, or carrying.**
   a. cat
   b. camel
   c. mongoose
   d. elephant
   e. goat
   f. llama
   g. chicken
   h. cheetah
3. The house cat was domesticated to solve a problem.
   a. Write the name of the country that had that problem.
   b. Which animals were causing that problem?
   c. How did cats solve the problem?
   d. How did the people show that they were grateful to the cats?
4. The mongoose has a special hunting use.
   a. Name the animal that mongooses kill.
   b. What can that animal's bite do to a person?

5. The claws of a hawk are called
   ● torches.   ● talons.   ● togas.
6. Name a product that each animal provides. Choose from **eggs, leather, or wool.**
   a. cow
   b. chicken
   c. sheep
7. Many animals have been used to carry things.
   a. Which South American animal was good at climbing mountains?
   b. Which large animal could easily push a truck over?
   c. Which inventions have made the carrying animals less important than they used to be?
8. Pretend that a farmer wants larger chicken eggs.
   a. The farmer would keep the chickens that laid the _____ eggs.
   ● smallest   ● most normal
   ● biggest
   b. After many generations, the new chickens would lay _____ eggs.
   ● smaller   ● the same
   ● bigger

PART C   Review Items

9. For each of the following animals, write **wild** or **domestic**.
   a. llama
   b. cobra
   c. mongoose
   d. chicken
   e. whale
   f. grasshopper
   g. camel
   h. goat

10. Use the words in the box to fill in the blanks or replace the underlined words.

suddenly said	dangled
obstacle	shabby
endurance	disgusting
spectators	frantically
magnificent	develop

   a. The tree that fell across the road was an _____ .

   b. It was very silent before Brian blurted out her name.
   c. If they have enough food, puppies grow quickly.
   d. Thousands of _____ gathered to see the event.
   e. The only coat Rob owned was in poor condition.
   f. When they entered the city, they saw a marvelous sight.
   g. She sat on the shore and _____ her feet in the water.
   h. Marta ran around the room very nervously looking for her paper.

PART D   Writing Assignment

What is your favorite domesticated animal?

Write at least **four** sentences that explain your answer.

Lesson 45

PART A   Word Lists

1	2	3	4
gnawed	fiction	flavor	**Vocabulary words**
fantasy	champion	comb	1. gnaw
bargain	selection	flavored	2. bargain
	nation	combed	3. shall
	domestication		4. pounce
	imagination		5. accept

PART B   Story Items

1. The man married the woman.
   a. What did they live in?
   b. What did they have inside the cave that gave off light?
2. The Wild Dog went to the cave.
   a. What food inside the cave interested the Wild Dog?

   b. What did the woman give the Wild Dog?
   c. What did the woman ask the Wild Dog to do in the daytime?
   d. What did the woman ask the Wild Dog to do at night?
   e. What was the Wild Dog's new name?

3. The woman got grass from a meadow.
   a. Why did she put the grass next to the fire?
   b. Which two animals liked the smell of the grass?
   c. Which of those two animals came to the cave first?
   d. What did the woman ask that animal to give her?
   e. What new name did the woman give that animal?
   f. What did the woman ask the Wild Horse to wear?
   g. What was the Wild Horse's new name?
4. Write which character could have said each sentence. Choose from the **woman,** the **cat,** the **cow,** the **dog,** or the **horse.**
   a. "I will give you this grass if you will be our servant."
   b. "That woman is very wise, but she is not as wise as I am."
   c. "I will wear that collar."
   d. "I will give you this bone if you will guard our cave."
   e. "I walk by myself, no matter where I go."
   f. "I will give you this grass if you will give me your milk."
   g. "I will give you my milk."
   h. "I will help you hunt."
5. Some of the things that happened in the story are **facts.**
   Some of the things that happened in the story are **fiction.**
   Write **fact** or **fiction** for each statement below.
   a. The dog was the first animal to be domesticated.
   b. It took only a couple of minutes to domesticate the dog.
   c. People lived in caves.
   d. The horse carried things for people.
   e. The cow was domesticated one day after the dog was domesticated.
   f. The animals talked to each other and talked to people.

PART C Review Items

6. **Use the words in the box to fill in the blanks or replace the underlined words.**

cooperating	guarantee
relative	gently push
develop	prey
ventured	prance
generation	caution
turf	grow

   a. Near the water jump, the <u>ground covered with grass</u> was very soft.
   b. The white horse began to _____ nervously.
   c. Children and their parents are not from the same <u>group of children who grow up together.</u>
   d. The lion crouched down and waited for its _____ to come closer.
   e. If you'd stop arguing and start <u>working together,</u> we could finish faster.
   f. They _____ into the dark cave.
   g. The lion is a _____ of the house cat.
   h. Can you <u>make sure</u> that Nellie will win the race?

PART D Writing Assignment

The cat in <u>The Cat that Walked by Himself</u> acts differently than the other animals.

Write at least **four** sentences that tell how the Cat is different.

Lesson 46

PART A   Word Lists

fantasy
flavored
accept
bargain

PART B   Neither–Nor

Use the words **neither** and **nor** to rewrite the following sentences.

1. The man was not happy and was not sad.
2. She would not play and would not sleep.
3. The boy would not smile and would not talk.
4. The dog could not fight and could not hunt.

PART C   Story Items

5. a. What work did the Dog say he would do?
   b. What work did the Horse say he would do?
   c. What work did the Cow say she would do?
6. When the Cat went to see the woman:
   a. The woman said that she had all the _____ and _____ that she needed.
   b. Who had seen the Cat hiding near the cave when the First Friend came to the cave?
   c. The Cat told the woman that she was wise and _____.
7. The woman and the Cat made a bargain.
   a. What would happen if the woman praised the Cat once?
   b. What would happen if the woman praised the Cat twice?
   c. What would happen if the woman praised the Cat three times?
8. What was new in the cave when the Cat decided that the time had come for him to move into the cave?
9. The Cat played with the baby outside the cave.
   a. What did the woman hear the baby do?
   b. Did she praise the Cat?
   c. So what did the Cat do?
10. a. After the Cat made the baby laugh, what did the Cat do with the baby?
    b. Did the woman praise the Cat for doing that?
    c. So what did the Cat do?
11. a. What did the Cat catch for the woman?
    b. Did the woman praise the Cat for doing that?
    c. So what did the Cat do?
12. a. Did the Cat have to be a friend or a servant to live in the cave?
    b. Did the Cat get a better deal than the Dog, the Cow, and the Horse?
13. Write which character could have said each sentence. Choose from the **cat** or the **woman.**
    a. "I am not a friend, and I am not a servant."
    b. "If I praise you, you may sit in the cave."
    c. "I am too busy cooking to deal with the baby."
    d. "I still walk by myself."
    e. "I must keep quiet, or I will praise him again."
    f. "You are very wise and very beautiful."
    g. "We do not need any more friends or servants."

PART D   Review Items

14. Use the words in the box to fill in the blanks or replace the underlined words.

officials	mock
endurance	sleek
made sure	strained
cooperate	keen

a. Lorenzo _____ with all his might and lifted the table.

b. The captain guaranteed that they would have a smooth trip.

c. Sophie decided to _____ and build a shed with the others.

d. She brushed the horse until his coat was very smooth.

e. The hawk has very _____ eyesight.

PART E   Writing Assignment

The story describes the domestication of the dog and the cat.

Write at least **four** sentences that tell how those animals were domesticated in the story.

Lesson 47

PART A   Word Lists

1	2	3
Warren	merchant	**Vocabulary words**
Alice	voyage	**1.** toss and turn
Whittington	observe	**2.** stroll
	threaten	**3.** stammer
	unbearable	**4.** fetch
		5. transport
		6. coach

PART B   Neither–Nor

Use the words **neither** and **nor** to rewrite the following sentences.

1. He could not swim and he could not dive.

2. She was not happy and she was not sad.

3. They could not walk and they could not run.

4. The woman could not sew and she could not cook.

PART C   Story Items

5. a. The story takes place about
      _____ hundred years ago.
   b. The trading merchants bought
      goods in one country. Where would
      they try to sell their goods?
6. At the beginning of the story, Dick
   came to a city.
   a. Which city?
   b. Which country is that city in?
   c. Who came to the city with Dick?
   d. That person said that the city had
      something marvelous. What was
      that?
   e. What happened to that person
      shortly after they arrived?
   f. Why did Dick begin to beg?
   g. Which character took Dick to his
      house?
7. a. Which character gave Dick a
      difficult time?
   b. Why didn't Dick get much sleep at
      night?
8. a. What did Dick find on the street?
   b. What did Dick buy?
   c. What did Dick do with it?
9. a. Mister Warren asked each servant
      to give him something. What was
      Mr. Warren going to do with those
      things?
   b. What was Mr. Warren going to do
      with the money he got for each
      thing?
   c. What did the cook give to Mister
      Warren?
   d. What did Dick give to Mister
      Warren?
10. What did Dick decide to do on the
    night that the mice came back?
11. Dick sat on a rock outside London.
    a. What did Dick hear?
    b. What did Dick believe would
       happen someday?
    c. So where did Dick return?

PART D   Review Items

12. Some of the things that happened in
    The Cat that Walked by Himself are
    facts, and other things are fiction.
    Write fact or fiction for each
    statement.
    a. Wild animals live in the woods.
    b. Wild horses can be domesticated in
       five minutes.
    c. Roast sheep smells good to a wild
       dog.
    d. The cat and the dog talk to each
       other.
    e. A cat can make some babies laugh.
    f. A cat catches mice.
    g. A cat talks to a woman.
13. Use the words in the box to fill in the
    blanks or replace the underlined
    words.

relatives	very smooth	shabby
dangled	marvelous	prancing
turf	wildly	

    a. There were five magnificent white
       horses hitched to the carriage.
    b. The deer looked shiny and sleek.
    c. After they escaped, they ran
       frantically to the river.
    d. His arms were loose and they
       _____ at his side.
    e. Her uncles and aunts and other
       members of the same family were at
       the picnic.

PART E   Writing Assignment

In some places, a cat would be worth a
lot of money.

Write at least **four** sentences that
describe such a place.

Lesson 48

PART A Word Lists

1
miserable
whirring
Yukon
Juneau
glacier

2
imagination
fiction
domestication
champion
selection
solution

3
purchase
voyage
palace
merchant

4
Vocabulary words
1. stammer
2. pounce
3. stroll
4. gnaw
5. accept

5
Vocabulary words
1. give credit
2. elect
3. college
4. brass
5. impatient

6
Vocabulary words
1. midday
2. bill
3. hatch
4. modest

PART B Story Items

1. Mister Warren's ship got lost.
   a. What made the ship go way off course to the west?
   b. What made the ship go north?
   c. What did the ship finally reach?
2. Why did Mister Warren leave the cat on the ship?
3. The queen served dinner.
   a. What came out of the walls?
   b. What did those animals do to the food?
   c. What did the queen promise to fill Mr. Warren's ship with if he solved that problem?
   d. What did Mister Warren get to solve that problem?
4. Mister Warren came back to England.
   a. How many carts did the gold fill?
   b. What did Dick first try to do with his riches?
   c. Name two people Dick gave gold to.
5. a. Name two ways Dick was different after he went shopping.
   b. Who did Dick marry?
   c. Which job did Dick have three times?
6. Some parts of Dick Whittington are **fact,** and some parts are **fiction.** Write **fact** or **fiction** for each statement.
   a. Dick Whittington was an orphan.
   b. Somebody gave a ship full of gold for Dick Whittington's cat.
   c. Dick Whittington was Mayor of London three times.
   d. Dick Whittington married Alice Warren.
   e. Mister Warren met a queen who lived on a strange island.
   f. Mister Warren was a traveling merchant.

PART C   Review Items

7. Write which character each statement describes. Choose from **Alice**, the **cook**, **Dick**, the **queen**, or **Mister Warren**.
   a. This character asked his servants for things to sell.
   b. This character made Dick work from dawn to dusk.
   c. This character slept in the attic with mice.
   d. This character married Dick.
   e. This character was bothered by mice each time dinner was served.

8. You read a story about a horse.
   a. What was the horse's name?
   b. Who rode the horse?
   c. Which blacksmith trained the horse?
   d. Near which city did the horse win the Grand National Steeplechase Championship?

9. **Use the words in the box to fill in the blanks or replace the underlined words.**

work together	venture	keen
frantically	caution	prey
guarantee	strained	

   a. The animals ran around <u>wildly</u> inside their cages.
   b. Can you <u>make sure</u> that the car would not break down?
   c. She was afraid to _____ down the dark tunnel.
   d. The mouse didn't know that it was the _____ of a large hawk.
   e. Her hearing was so _____ that she could hear things that were far off.

PART D   Writing Assignment

What do you think would happen if there were no cats in the world?

Write at least **four** sentences that explain your answer.

Lesson 49

PART A   Word Lists

1	2	3	4 Vocabulary words	5 Vocabulary words
eventually	scramble	Dawson	1. give credit	1. eventually
rustle	grumble	Skagway	2. elect	2. scrambled
descend	middle		3. brass	3. disgraceful
boulder	comfortable		4. impatient	4. lean
treacherous	tumble		5. modest	5. vivid
	waddle			6. descended
	mantel			7. treacherous

PART B   Review Items

1. Rewrite the following sentences using the words **neither** and **nor.**
   a. She is not short and she is not lean.
   b. He was not cunning and he was not smart.

2. **Use the words in the box to fill in the blanks or replace the underlined words.**

hung loosely	straining	fetch
cooperate	ventured	keen
relatives	transport	

   a. He was getting tired and he was _____ to keep up with the others.
   b. At first the puppies fought over the food, but later they learned to work together.
   c. The old wizard had a very _____ understanding of their problems.
   d. He offered to _____ the family across the desert.
   e. Shelly taught her dog to _____ things that she threw.

PART C   Writing Assignment

Write a poem about an animal that you like. Describe how the animal looks and explain why you like the animal. Your poem does not have to rhyme.

Lesson 50

PART A   Word Lists

1	2	3	4
ugly	volcano	**Vocabulary words**	**Vocabulary words**
quietly	volcanic	1. scramble	1. rustling
doubtfully	glacier	2. lean	2. flounder
hardly	Juneau	3. eventually	3. miserable
bitterly	Yukon	4. disgraceful	4. crest
exactly		5. treacherous	5. boulder
		6. descend	6. rapids
		7. vivid	

PART B   Story Items

1. **a.** In what year was gold discovered in Northern Canada?
   b. Near which town was it discovered?
2. Pretend you are traveling to Dawson. Write the name of the first city you go to.
3. You see a large glacier. What color is the tip of the glacier?

4. **a.** What town do you come to after Juneau?
   b. Is that town in Alaska or Canada?
   c. Why wouldn't you want to buy things in that town?
   d. From that town, you follow a mountain trail until you reach a _____ that is nearly one hundred miles long.

PART C   Review Items

5. Write **fact** or **fiction** for each item.
   a. A mother duck must continue to sit on eggs.
   b. A mother duck talks to neighbors.
   c. The egg of a swan is bigger than the egg of a duck.
   d. Hunters shoot geese.
   e. Ducks fly south in the fall.
   f. Geese talk to ducks.
6. **Use the words in the box to fill in the blanks or replace the underlined words.**

endurance	cooperate
impatient	shabby
coaches	accept
strolled	transport

   a. The smart person is the one who learns to _____ with others.
   b. They hoped that the raft would _____ them across the river.
   c. They walked slowly along the riverbank.

   d. The engine pulled five splendid _____.
   e. She had been wanting to go swimming for a week and she was _____.

PART D   Writing Assignment

Pick a place that you know well. Then write a paragraph that describes what it looks like. Your paragraph should give a good picture of the place.

Make your paragraph at least **four** sentences long.

Lesson 51

Vocabulary words
1. murmur
2. whittling
3. sneer
4. coil
5. exchanged
6. flickered
7. hurl
8. limp

PART B   Story Items

1. **a.** In what year was gold discovered in Northern Canada?
   b. Near which town was it discovered?
2. At Juneau, you see a great glacier. What color is the tip of the glacier?
3. **a.** What's the name of the river you finally reach?
   b. Which part of the river trip is frightening?
   c. Can you ride your boat down all the rapids?
   d. How long can it take you to go one mile on land?
4. At last you reach a great valley. What's the name of that valley?
5. Name five animals that you see on your trip.

PART C   Review Items

6. Rewrite the sentences using the words **neither** and **nor.**
   a. I would not run and I would not jump.
   b. They are not laughing and they are not singing.

7. Write whether each statement describes **Dick Whittington, The Cat That Walked by Himself,** or **The Ugly Duckling.**
   a. The main character made a good bargain.
   b. Some of the characters lived in a cave.
   c. The main character was a boy.
   d. The story took place in London, England.
   e. The major character was a bird.
   f. The story ended in a pool of water.
   g. The story told how some animals were domesticated.
   h. The story told how a character became rich.
   i. The story told about a character who did not know what he looked like.
8. Write which color each thing is.
   a. Emerald City
   b. Glinda's dress
   c. The Quadlings
   d. Munchkin houses
   e. The Winkies
   f. Swans
   g. The tips of glaciers
   h. Nighthawk

9. **Use the words in the box to fill in the blanks or replace the underlined words.**

full of attention	terrible
give credit	stroll
nudged	fetch
college	coach
hurried	

a. Go _____ the newspaper for me.

b. After he graduated from high school, he attended _____.

c. The _____ was pulled by four black horses.

d. He did most of the work but nobody would _____ to him.

e. Breaking the window is a disgraceful thing to do.

f. They scrambled away when they heard the lion advancing.

PART D   Writing Assignment

Would you want to go all the way to Dawson to look for gold?

Write at least **four** sentences that explain your answer.

Lesson 52

PART A   Word Lists

1	2	3 Vocabulary words	4 Vocabulary words
overhead	mine	1. flicker	1. lingered on
hillslope	miner	2. sneer	2. buds
waterfall	baggage	3. murmur	3. staggered
motionless	cricket	4. hurl	4. sap
downstream	Thornton	5. coil	5. runners
	exchanged	6. miserable	
		7. reflection	

PART B   Story Items

1. a. Along which river did the story Buck take place?
   b. What season was it?
   c. When did the sun rise?
   d. When did the sun set?
2. The river was dangerous because
   • the ice was thawing.
   • the ice was thick.
   • the tide was coming in.
3. A dog sled came into John Thornton's camp.
   a. How many men were with the sled?
   b. What place were they trying to reach?
   c. What kind of condition were the dogs in?
   d. What did Thornton warn the men about?
   e. Did the men follow Thornton's advice?
4. a. What command did the man give his dog team when he wanted them to move forward?
   b. Write the name of the lead dog.
   c. What did the man do to the dogs when they did not follow his command?
   d. Which dog still refused to follow the man's command?
5. Why had Buck sensed disaster?
6. a. Who jumped on the man?
   b. Why did he do that?
   c. What did Thornton knock out of the man's hand?
   d. What did Thornton cut?

7. What terrible thing happened to the sled after it started again?
8. Write which character could have made each statement. Choose from **Thornton** or the **driver.**
   a. "They told us we couldn't make it, but here we are."
   b. "We'll go on to Dawson."
   c. "I'll beat any dog that doesn't obey me."
   d. "This fool will not follow my advice."
   e. "I cannot stand to see that dog suffer."
   f. "I wouldn't dare to go on that ice."
   g. "I'll make it to Dawson."

PART C   Review Items

9. **Use the words in the box to fill in the blanks or replace the underlined words.**

eventually	elected	numb
gave credit	hatch	lean
walked slowly	fetch	terrible
rustling	modest	

   a. Martin whistled as he strolled through the park.
   b. She was too _____ to say that she had earned the best score on the test.
   c. The other members _____ Leon, president of the club.

d. She could be very funny but her teachers thought that her behavior was <u>disgraceful</u>.

e. She planted seeds and <u>at last</u> plants grew.

f. The goose sat on her eggs and waited for them to _____.

g. The dog was so _____ that you could see all of his ribs.

h. They heard the deer _____ through the trees.

PART D   **Writing Assignment**

Name some things that are different when you follow the Yukon during the winter rather than the summer.

Write at least **four** sentences.

Lesson 53

PART A   **Word Lists**

1	**2**	**3**	**4**
Hans	tumble	**Vocabulary words**	**Vocabulary words**
tolerate	grumble	1. lingered on	1. recover
haunt	muscle	2. stagger	2. embrace
naked	scramble		3. ideal
	comfortable		4. affection
			5. haunt
			6. tolerated
			7. naked
			8. grapple

PART B   **Main Idea Sentences**

Mary

Tom

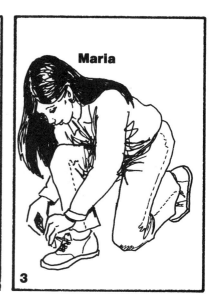

Maria

PART C   Story Items

4. John Thornton had been in the tent for two months.
   a. Who were his partners?
   b. Why had his partners left him there?
   c. What were his partners making?
   d. What were they going to use that thing for?
5. a. How did John Thornton treat Buck?
   b. What strange way did Buck have of showing his love for Thornton?
   c. Why was Buck afraid that Thornton would leave him?
   d. How did Buck act toward other people?
6. a. Where were Buck and Thornton when Thornton gave a silly command?
   b. What command did Thornton give to Buck?
   c. What did Buck try to do?
   d. Who stopped Buck?
7. The men and Buck left the next day.
   a. What was the name of the river they went down?
   b. What did they use to go down the river?
   c. What town did they go to?
8. Two men were having a fight.
   a. Why did Thornton step between the two men?
   b. What did one of the men do to Thornton?
   c. What did Buck do to the man?
   d. Why did Buck do that?
   e. Why did the miners set Buck free?
   f. Why did Buck's name spread through every mining camp along the Yukon?
9. Write whether each statement describes **Buck, Thornton,** or **Hans.**
   a. He had frozen his feet.
   b. He had saved a dog's life.
   c. He almost jumped off a cliff.
   d. He would do anything for his master.
   e. He would gently bite somebody's hand.
   f. He had gone up the Yukon to build a raft.
   g. He was not a close friend of the dog.

PART D   Review Items

10. **Use the words in the box to fill in the blanks or replace the underlined words.**

at last	floundered	sleek
miserable	scrambled	plod
gave credit	elect	vivid
treacherous	modest	

   a. Cheryl didn't win the race, but they _____ to her for trying.
   b. The deer <u>hurried</u> out of the pen.
   c. Molly did not accept a medal for saving the boy's life because she was too _____.
   d. Taming tigers is a <u>very dangerous</u> job.
   e. They voted to _____ a new president of the company.
   f. Jeremy's headache made him feel _____.
   g. She _____ in the middle of the slippery ice.
   h. Street signs must be a _____ color, so they can be seen from a distance.

PART E   Writing Assignment

Thornton ordered Buck to jump off the cliff because he wanted to show that Buck would do anything for him.

Write at least **three** other ways that Thornton could have shown that Buck was loyal.

Lesson 54

PART A Word Lists

1	2	3	4	5
guilty	particularly	**Vocabulary words**	**Vocabulary words**	**Vocabulary words**
Eldorado	instantly	1. affection	1. mountain pass	1. jutted out
jutted	desperately	2. grapple	2. strangle	2. reared up
pistol	apparently	3. tolerate	3. flushed	3. stretch
ashore		4. recover	4. guilty	4. clutched
rouse		5. embrace		
lunge		6. haunt		
		7. ideal		

PART B Main Idea Sentences

Write the main idea sentence for each row of pictures below.

PART C   Story Items

4. This part of the story begins on the Forty Mile Creek.
   a. Which character was in the boat?
   b. Which three characters were on the shore?
   c. What were the men on shore using to guide the boat?
5. a. What did the boat hit that made it flip over?
   b. What happened to John Thornton?
   c. What did Buck do when the boat flipped?
   d. What part of Buck did Thornton hold onto?
   e. Which was faster, their progress toward the shore, or their progress downstream?
   f. When Thornton crashed into a _____, he let go of Buck.
6. Buck swam back to the shore.
   a. Who was waiting for him there?
   b. What did Hans and Pete attach to Buck?
   c. Then what did they do?
   d. Did Buck reach Thornton the first time?
   e. Who pulled Buck back to shore?
   f. What condition was Buck in when he reached the shore?
7. Buck was thrown in again.
   a. Did he swim farther out the second time?
   b. Who did Buck ram into?
   c. How did they get back to the shore?
   d. Which bones of Buck's were broken?
8. Some men were talking in the Eldorado Hotel.
   a. What were they bragging about?
   b. How many pounds did Thornton say that Buck could pull?
   c. Write the name of the character who said that Buck couldn't do that.
   d. What prize did that character offer Thornton?
   e. Was Thornton certain that Buck could pull the sled?

PART D   Review Items

9. Use the words in the box to fill in the blanks or replace the underlined words.

very large rock	staggered	crest
eventually	flounder	elect
impatiently	miserable	modest
sound	rustled	
reflection	rapids	

   a. The dog barked _____ while waiting to be let out.
   b. For years things were very bad, but they _____ changed.
   c. Steve cried because he felt _____.
   d. The mice _____ through the underbrush.
   e. The _____ on the windows hurt her eyes.
   f. The river was very fast and had many _____.
   g. They could see for miles from the top of the mountain.
   h. Nobody could move the boulder.
   i. The tired horse stumbled and fell.
   j. In the distance, we could hear the low murmur of the wind.

PART E   Writing Assignment

Describe some of the things that might happen to Buck when he tries to pull that heavy load.

Write at least **four** sentences.

Lesson 55

PART A   Word Lists

1
admiration
condition
conversation
affection

2
Vocabulary words
1. quiver
2. grate

3
Vocabulary words
1. rouse
2. witnessed
3. lunged
4. outskirts

PART B

Vocabulary Sentences

1. He was sleeping soundly and even when his mother shook him, he would not <u>rouse</u>.
2. Most of the people who <u>witnessed</u> the race saw Tina fall down.
3. The lion gathered all its strength and suddenly <u>lunged</u> forward.
4. He wanted to live very near the city, so he bought a place on the <u>outskirts</u> of the city.

PART C   Main Idea Sentences

Write the main idea sentences for pictures **1, 2** and **3.** Then write the main idea sentence for the row of pictures in item 4.

1.

2.

3.

4.

PART D   Story Items

5. The men poured into the street.
   a. What season was it in this part of the story?
   b. IIow many degrees below zero was it outside?
   c. What had happened to the sled's runners as the sled sat in the cold?
   d. How many dogs normally pulled the sled?
      ● two   ● ten   ● twenty
   e. What objects were on the sled?
6. a. What kind of condition was Buck in?
   b. Did he have any fat on him?
   c. How many pounds did he weigh?
   d. Why did the tall man offer to buy Buck?
7. Thornton talked to Buck.
   a. What did Buck do to Thornton's hand?
   b. What was Thornton's first command to Buck?

   c. In which direction did Buck go?
   d. What noise did the runners make?
   e. What was Thornton's second command to Buck?
   f. In which direction did Buck go?
   g. What happened to the runners after Buck obeyed the second command?
8. Thornton gave a third command.
   a. What was Thornton's third command to Buck?
   b. In which direction did Buck go?
   c. How far did Buck have to move the sled?
   d. What did the pile of firewood mark?
   e. How did the men respond when Buck pulled the load?
   f. Why did the tall man offer Thornton more money for Buck?

PART E   Review Items

9. Use the words in the box to fill in the blanks or replace the underlined words.

fetch	terrible	sneer
murmur	hugged	hatch
exchanged	impatient	vivid
floundered	recover	rapids
college		

a. The king had done some very cruel and disgraceful things.

b. When the shells start to crack, the eggs are about to _____.

c. She tried to swim but _____ in the breaking waves.

d. She painted an attractive picture with colors that were very

_____.

e. The boat tipped when it went over the _____.

f. I like to sit in the forest and listen to the sound of the animals.

g. The wizard's evil laugh and mocking smile frightened her.

h. The little girl traded the jump rope for a coloring book.

i. She sat and rested to get back her strength from the long run.

j. The friends embraced each other happily.

PART F   Writing Assignment

How was Buck different at the end of the story than he was at the beginning of the story?

Write at least **four** sentences.

Lesson 56

PART A   Word Lists

1
Mount Whitney
Los Angeles
scenery
Pennsylvania
barren

2
Mount Shasta
Glen Ellen
groove
grove
combine
combined

3
Vocabulary words
1. guilty
2. grate
3. lunged
4. rouse
5. outskirts
6. witness

4
Vocabulary words
1. scenery
2. barren
3. splinters
4. topple
5. shredded

PART B
Vocabulary Sentences

1. He stood outside the cabin and looked at the beautiful scenery that surrounded it.
2. The hills were barren with no trees and no bushes.
3. He hit the wooden block with an ax and the block became a pile of splinters.
4. They sawed through the great tree and slowly it began to topple.
5. The lion clawed the scarecrow's coat until the coat was completely shredded.

PART C　　Main Idea Sentences

Write the main idea sentence for the row of
pictures and for pictures **2** and **3.**

1.

2.

3.

PART D   Story Items

4. About how far is it from the northern border of California to the southern border?

5. When you go up a mountain, the plants change the way they change when you go _____.
   - north ● east
   - west ● south

6. a. A mountain is coldest at _____ feet.
      - 1,000 ● 7,000 ● 12,000
   b. A mountain is hottest at _____ feet.
      - 1,000 ● 7,000 ● 12,000

7. What's the name of the tallest mountain in California?

8. How high up do you have to go up a mountain in California before there are no more trees?

9. Which part of the very high mountains has snow all year round?

10. Why are trees at 10,000 feet smaller than trees at 1,000 feet?

11. a. What's the name of the very tall trees that grow in California?
    b. How tall are the largest of those trees?
    c. That's as tall as a building that is _____ stories tall.

12. a. What's the name of the place you'll read about in the next story?
    b. Name two types of trees that grow near that place.
    c. That place is forty miles north of a large California city. Write the name of that city.

PART E   Review Items

13. Use the words in the box to fill in the blanks or replace the underlined words.

felt very bad	tolerated	threw
very dangerous	excellent	sneer
reflections	eventually	lean
affection	boulder	rapids

a. The river will _____ change its course.
b. Pat was very _____ and ran well.
c. The swans looked at their _____ in the water.
d. They started up the steep trail to the top of the treacherous mountain.
e. There was a very large rock in the field among the smaller rocks.
f. She hurled her shoe against the wall.
g. The sunny day was ideal for a picnic.
h. She felt a lot of love for her old friend.
i. The movie was bad but they put up with it.

PART F   Writing Assignment

Which state would you most like to live in?

Write at least **four** sentences that explain your answer.

Lesson 57

PART A   Word Lists

1
Madge Irvine
Oregon
bristle
squirm
miracle

2
effortless
blackberry
outskirts
meadowlark

3
Walt
starve
starvation
brow

4
Vocabulary words
1. splinters
2. topple
3. scenery
4. shredded
5. barren

5
Vocabulary words
1. effortlessly
2. spring
3. fangs
4. miracle

6
Vocabulary words
1. soiled
2. meadowlark
3. forelegs
4. halt
5. hardships

PART B
Vocabulary Sentences

1. After he rolled on the wet grass and dirt, his pants were <u>soiled</u>.
2. The <u>meadowlark</u> spread its wings, raised its head, and began to sing.
3. A dog has two hind legs and two <u>forelegs</u>.
4. He ordered his dog to stop and the dog <u>halted</u> immediately.
5. He experienced many <u>hardships</u>— hunger, pain, and long hours of hard work.

PART C   Main Idea Sentences

Write the main idea sentence for the row of pictures and for pictures **2, 3,** and **4.**

1.

2.

3.

4.

PART D   Story Items

5. In which state does this story take place?

6. Wolf had come to the Irvines three years before.
   a. How did they know that the dog was not really a wolf?
   b. When Wolf arrived, was he in good shape or poor shape?
   c. How friendly was he when he arrived?
   d. What did Wolf always do when he felt better?
   e. In which direction would he always go?

7. Walt took a business trip.
   a. In which direction was Walt going?
   b. Who did Walt see that made him get off at the next station?

8. a. What did Walt put around Wolf's neck?
   b. Walt did that so people would know
      • where to send Wolf.
      • Wolf's name.
      • where Glen Ellen is.

9. a. What state did Wolf reach on the longest run that he made?
   b. How many miles would Wolf cover on the first day?
      • 50   • 150   • 250
   c. How many miles did he cover on each day after the first day?
      • 100   • 200   • 300

10. Wolf accepted the Irvines at last.
    a. What kind of dog did Mrs. Johnson think Wolf was?
    b. What noise did Wolf make when the north wind blew?

11. a. The Irvines figured that Wolf must have come to Glen Ellen from the
       _____.
       • north   • east
       • west   • south
    b. What made them think that he had come from that direction?

12. a. What was the name of the man the Irvines met in the clearing?
    b. What color was that character's clothes?
    c. Was that character weak or strong?
    d. Where was that character from?

e. Who was that character going to see?

13. Wolf never did something that most dogs do all the time. What was that?

PART E   Review Items

14. Rewrite these sentences using the words **neither** and **nor**.
    a. Rover would not bark and he would not bite.
    b. The baby is not crawling and she is not crying.

15. **Use the words in the box to fill in the blanks or replace the underlined words.**

treacherous	impatient	naked
disgraceful	wrestled	top
reflection	guilty	vivid
descended	modest	sneer

   a. The child was very _____ for her father to come home from work.
   b. His friends thought the horrible things he did were <u>terrible</u>.
   c. The icy road was slippery and <u>very dangerous</u>.
   d. The climbers rested when they got to the <u>crest</u> of the hill.
   e. Joel didn't like them and looked at them with a <u>mean smile</u>.
   f. The wind blew all the leaves off the tree, and left the branches <u>bare</u>.
   g. The two bears growled and <u>grappled</u> fiercely with each other.
   h. The children <u>came down</u> the ladder.
   i. The cat was the _____ one, because it had broken the vase.

PART F   Writing Assignment

You know which direction Wolf always goes. Tell where you think Wolf was coming from when he reached the Irvine's cabin. Tell where you think he was trying to go. Then tell why you think he wanted to go there.

Write at least **four** sentences.

Lesson 58

PART A   Word Lists

1
potato
erect
decisive
misery

2
forelegs
footpads
hardship
heartbreaking

3
droopy
cripple
tense
intense
owl
crippled

4
Vocabulary words
1. miracle
2. spring
3. fangs
4. effortlessly
5. halt
6. forelegs
7. hardships

5
Vocabulary words
1. erect
2. reappear
3. decisive
4. misery
5. tussle
6. intense

PART B   Main Idea Passages

Write the main idea sentence for each of these passages.

1. Roses grow in the summer.
   Pansies grow in the summer.
   Buttercups grow in the summer.

2. Flowers produce oxygen.
   Trees produce oxygen.
   Grass produces oxygen.

3. Trucks need gasoline.
   Cars need gasoline.
   Motorcycles need gasoline.

PART C   Main Idea Sentences

Write the main idea sentence for picture **4** and the row of pictures.

4.

5.

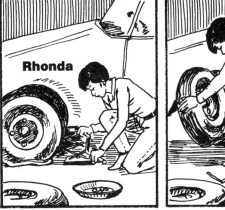  

PART D   Story Items

6. Wolf came into the clearing.
   a. Which person did Wolf go up to?
   b. What noise did Wolf make?
   c. Why were Madge and Walt surprised by this noise?
7. a. Who claimed that Wolf was his dog?
   b. What name did that character call the dog?
   c. How did that character prove that the dog was his?
   d. Write the **two** commands that character gave Wolf.
8. a. Where did Skiff want to take Wolf?
   b. Where would life be easier for Wolf—in California or in the other place?
   c. In which place did Skiff think that Wolf would prefer to live?
   d. Why was Wolf used to life in that place?
9. Write **two** reasons why Madge thought that California was better for Wolf than the Yukon.
10. a. At first, did Walt agree that Wolf was Miller's dog?
    b. Why didn't Walt think that Miller's commands proved anything?
    c. Why did Madge step between the two men?
11. a. Did Madge think that Wolf belonged to Skiff?
    b. Write **two** reasons why she felt that way.
    c. Did everybody finally agree about which person really owned Wolf?

PART E   Review Items

12. **Use the words in the box to fill in the blanks or replace the underlined words.**

got its strength back	hurled
walked slowly	coach
clear and easy to see	trade
put up with	ideal
miserable	clutched
transport	

   a. The puppy was lonely and felt <u>very bad</u>.
   b. Everything was <u>vivid</u> in the sunlight.
   c. Theresa asked if she could <u>exchange</u> the dress for another one.
   d. Jason <u>threw</u> the rock into the water.
   e. At first the cat was exhausted; however, it <u>recovered</u> within an hour.
   f. Marlene was an _____ basketball player because she was tall and fast.
   g. The horse <u>tolerated</u> the heat.
   h. Sylvia didn't drown because she _____ the side of the boat.

PART F   Writing Assignment

Pretend that Wolf is your dog. Miller is trying to take the dog away from you. You agree that Wolf probably belonged to Miller years ago. But you feel that Wolf is your dog now.

Write at least **three** things you would tell Miller to prove that you own Wolf.

Lesson 59

PART A Word Lists

1
reluctant
determination
sensitive
ma'am

2
curled
gurgled
curve
further

3
picnic
runt
health
healthy
ache
aching

4
Vocabulary words
1. reappear
2. decisive
3. misery
4. intense
5. tussle
6. erect

5
Vocabulary words
1. litter
2. reluctant
3. limp
4. crippled
5. sensitive
6. determination

6
Vocabulary words
1. loafed
2. afford
3. operated

PART B Vocabulary Sentences

1. He was so lazy that he always <u>loafed</u> when he was supposed to be working.
2. She had very little money so she could not <u>afford</u> a new car.
3. The doctors <u>operated</u> on her crippled leg, and now she can walk much better.

PART C Main Idea Passages

Write the main idea sentence for each of these passages.

1. Wild deer live in the jungle.
   Wild tigers live in the jungle.
   Wild apes live in the jungle.

2. Vanessa dug a hole.
   Then Vanessa picked up a tree.
   Vanessa put the tree in the hole.

3. Maria goes to Jefferson School everyday.
   Henry goes to Jefferson School everyday.
   Lisa goes to Jefferson School everyday.

4. The weeds in the fields come up to your waist.
   The cornstalks in the fields come up to your waist.
   The wheat in the fields comes up to your waist.

PART D   Main Idea Sentences

Write the main idea sentence for the row of
pictures and for picture **6.**

5.

6.

PART E   Story Items

7. **a.** Who asked Skiff to consider Wolf's feelings?
   b. How did that person want Wolf to feel, no matter where he was?
   c. In which place did that person think Wolf wanted to be?
8. **a.** Who came up with a way to let the dog make a choice?
   b. What would the Irvines do?
   c. What would Skiff do?
   d. Who would call the dog?
   e. Who would the dog stay with if the dog remained in the meadow?
   f. Who would the dog stay with if the dog went down the trail?
9. **a.** Why did Wolf grab on to Skiff's hand?
   b. Why did Wolf grab Walt's hand?
   c. Did Wolf's plan work?
10. **a.** Who was the last person Wolf came up to?
    b. After Miller was out of view, Madge smiled at Walt. Why?
11. When Wolf started to make decisive movements, the Irvines knew something.
    a. What did they know?
    b. Why didn't Madge call out to Wolf?
    c. Where was Wolf going at the end of the story?

PART F   Review Items

12. Rewrite these sentences using the words **neither** and **nor**.
    a. The table is not tall and it is not made of wood.
    b. Her dress was not long and it was not pretty.
13. Use the words in the box to fill in the blanks or replace the underlined words.

affection	barren	lunged
impatient	sneer	saw
miserable	scenery	top
eventually	guilty	miracle
embraced		

   a. Dorothy will <u>at last</u> get back to Kansas.
   b. The man felt <u>very bad</u> from walking home <u>in the rain</u>.
   c. Judy <u>hugged</u> her mother lovingly.
   d. Greg <u>showed</u> his cat a lot of love and _____.
   e. The criminals were _____ of robbery.
   f. He <u>witnessed</u> them eating their lunch.
   g. Alex took a fast run and _____ across the streambed.
   h. The _____ in the little valley was magnificent.
   i. After the hungry goats had grazed, the fields were <u>bare</u>.
   j. It was a _____ that the man was not hurt after falling five stories.

PART G   Writing Assignment

Pretend that you are Wolf at the end of the story. Tell some sad things that you are feeling. Write some of the things you are looking forward to.

Write at least **four** sentences.

Lesson 60

PART A Word Lists

1
North Carolina
coax
Yodeler

2
cripple
incredible
snuggle
tickle
tussle
tumble

3
Vocabulary words
1. sensitive
2. reluctant
3. limp
4. determination
5. litter
6. crippled
7. loafed
8. afford

PART B Main Idea Passages

Write the main idea sentence for each of these passages.

1. Maria looked through a lens.
   Then Maria said, "Smile."
   Then Maria pushed a button on her camera.

2. The dog dug a hole.
   The dog put a bone in the hole.
   The dog filled the hole with dirt.

3. Tina put the pencil into the sharpener.
   Then Tina turned the handle.
   Tina pulled the pencil out of the sharpener.

4. Some hammers are made of steel.
   Some saws are made of steel.
   Some screwdrivers are made of steel.

5. All robins have feathers.
   All pigeons have feathers.
   All penguins have feathers.

PART C Story Items

6. a. How big was Martha compared to her brothers and sisters?
    b. What did Julie's father want to do with Martha shortly after she was born?
    c. He called her a _____ .
    d. He kept only those puppies that were _____ .
    e. Who pleaded with him to keep Martha?
    f. Did her father finally agree?

7. a. Where did Julie keep Martha at night?
       • In the kennel
       • In her bedroom
       • In the meadow
    b. What did Julie use to feed Martha?
    c. How often did Julie feed Martha?

8. How long does it take for puppies to open their eyes?

9. **a.** Martha had an unusually keen sense. Which sense was that?
   b. Did Julie, her father, or anybody else know that Martha had this keen sense?
10. Which smells did Martha prefer at first, the smells of the other dogs or the smell of Julie?
11. Julie's father tested the puppies to see which would be strong hunters.
    a. He put them in a shallow _____.
    b. What did he put over the top of that thing?
    c. What did he put just outside of that thing?
    d. The best puppies are the ones that keep _____.
    e. What did Martha do?
12. Martha had an experience with her sense of smell in the meadow behind Julie's house.
    a. How old was Martha at that time?
    b. What had she been doing before she had that experience?
    c. What was the experience?

PART D   Review Items

13. **Use the words in the box to fill in the blanks or replace the underlined words.**

very dangerous	vivid	fell down
scrambling	halt	shredded
miserable	lunged	soiled
clutched	spring	scenery

a. The white shirt was _____ and stained.
b. Felix could recognize Nancy by the _____ colors of her sweater.
c. Allen tightly held her hand and did not let go.
d. The tiger _____ at the deer next to the tree.
e. From the top of the mountain, the _____ was very pretty.
f. The building leaned over more and more until one year it finally toppled.
g. Sandra tore up the letter into little pieces and threw it in the trash.
h. The pond got its water from an underground _____.
i. The soldiers stopped when the captain told them to stop.

PART E   Writing Assignment

Describe the smells you like the most. Then describe the smells you like the least.

Write at least **four** sentences.

Lesson 61

PART A   Word Lists

1	2	3	4
kennel	ledge	moist	**Vocabulary words**
quail	ridge	moisture	1. kennel
dwarf	edge	chill	2. ridge
Yodeler	nudge	chilly	3. ledge
		tearful	4. quail
			5. dwarf

PART B Main Idea Passages

Write the main idea sentence for each of the passages.

1. The bear in the cave slept for three months.
   The wolf in the cave slept for three months.
   The lion in the cave slept for three months.

2. Rowboats go in the water.
   Sailboats go in the water.
   Tugboats go in the water.

3. John swung a bat and ran around the bases.
   Later John threw a ball to first base.
   Later John caught a line drive.

4. The horses heard a gun go off.
   The horses jumped over nineteen barriers.
   At last the horses crossed the finish line.

PART C Story Items

5. a. A group of puppies that are born at the same time is called a

   _____.

   b. When young hounds hunt, they have a problem of staying on only one _____.
   c. What do they want to do?
   d. Who trained the young hounds?
   e. Did Martha go with her brothers and sisters?

6. a. What was the name of the best dog that Julie's father had in the kennel?
   b. Julie's father took that dog along when he trained the young hounds because that dog could show the others _____.

7. Julie's father had always dreamed of the day that one of his hounds would be able to track an animal over a particular place.
   a. Write the name of that place.
   b. Write one reason that hounds could not track over that place.
   c. How many dogs had tracked an animal over that place?

8. a. What kind of animal had Julie's father taken the hounds to track?
   b. Was Leader able to follow the scent on the rocky ridge?

9. One night, Julie and her mother were waiting for somebody to come home.
   a. Who was that?
   b. What season was it?
   c. Describe the weather.

10. Julie tried to keep Martha from bothering her.
    a. What was the first thing that Martha played with?
    b. Then Julie hid something from Martha. What did she hide?
    c. Why didn't it take Martha very long to find it?

11. Julie's father wasn't able to get home.
    a. Where had Julie's father gone?
    b. Why didn't he walk home?
    c. Who did he have close to him?
    d. Why?

12. Later, Julie saw something outside the window.
    a. What did she see?
    b. When the dogs from the litter came home, Julie and her mother knew something. What conclusion did they draw?

PART D   Review Items

13. Use the words in the box to fill in the blanks or replace the underlined words.

come back into sight	
very dangerous	miracle
hardships	officials
decisively	intense
witness	vivid
misery	lunged
afford	bare

a. The old stairs were full of holes and <u>treacherous</u>.

b. The people did not <u>see</u> the girl falling down.

c. There was nothing but sand across the <u>barren</u> desert.

d. When the dog made it through the snowstorm, people said it was a strange _____.

e. They ran out of food and suffered many other _____.

f. The seals dove into the water and their trainer waited for them to reappear.

g. Once Nick knew what he wanted to do, he went about the task _____.

h. The starving dog howled with _____.

i. The drowning man could not swim against the <u>very strong</u> current.

j. Because Edna was rich, she could _____ to go to the most expensive restaurants in town.

PART E   Writing Assignment

What do you think happened to Julie's father?

Write at least **four** sentences that explain your answer.

Lesson 62

PART A   Word Lists

1	2	3	4
Johnson	gong	**Vocabulary words**	**Vocabulary words**
receiver	possible	1. ledge	1. stocking cap
alert	possibilities	2. dwarf	2. down
	expected	3. quail	3. receiver
	unexpectedly	4. ridge	
	operation	5. kennel	
	Whitebirds		

PART B   Main Idea Passages

Write the main idea sentence for each of the passages.

1. The Atlantic Ocean is made of salt water.
The Pacific Ocean is made of salt water.
The Indian Ocean is made of salt water.

2. Los Angeles is in California.
Glen Ellen is in California.
San Francisco is in California.

3. Willie wrote a letter.
Willie put a stamp on the letter.
Willie put the letter in a mailbox.

4. Frank picked up the receiver.
Frank dialed seven numbers.
Frank said, "Hello."

PART C   Story Items

5. a. Julie's mother tried to call the
    _____ .
   b. Why didn't she succeed?
   c. What did Julie's mother do next?
6. Write the name of one thing that Julie
   was supposed to do.
7. a. What time was it when Julie
      decided to do something to find her
      father?
      ● midnight
      ● one o'clock in the morning
      ● eleven o'clock at night
   b. Who was going to help Julie find
      her father?
8. After Julie put Martha on a leash, she
   held something out for Martha to
   smell.
   a. What did Julie hold?
   b. Did Martha understand what to do
      at first?
9. Martha picked up a scent. What left
   that scent?
10. The way Martha was moving told
    Julie what Martha was tracking.
    a. Martha was moving in a
       _____ .
    b. What did Julie do to get Martha on
       the right track?
11. a. Was Martha able to track Julie's
       father?
    b. Which would Martha prefer
       tracking, Julie's father or a deer?
12. a. When Martha tracked animals,
       what sound did she make?
       ● a whine   ● a howl
       ● a short bark
    b. When Martha was tracking Julie's
       father, what sound did she make?
       ● a whine   ● a howl
       ● a short bark
13. At last, Julie made a difficult decision
    because she couldn't move very fast.
    a. Why couldn't Julie move fast?
    b. What did Julie decide to do?
    c. What was Julie afraid that Martha
       might do?
    d. What did Julie do just before she
       released Martha?

PART D   Review Items

14. **Use the words in the box to fill in the
    blanks or replace the underlined
    words.**

put up with	spring
determination	stop
decisive	saw
sensitive	toppled
reluctant to	afford
wrestle	

   a. When Bob pushed him, he <u>fell</u>
      over.
   b. The thirsty traveler drank from a
      cool _____ .
   c. The car slowed down until it came
      to a <u>halt</u>.
   d. They rented an inexpensive house
      because they could not
      _____ anything else.
   e. Nobody could change Amy's mind,
      she was _____ about it.
   f. The cat was _____ jump
      into the cold water.
   g. His ears were _____ to very
      high sounds.
   h. The tiger showed great _____
      to get out of the cage.

PART E   Writing Assignment

Julie has decided to do something very
dangerous.

Write at least **four** sentences that
explain what problems Julie might
have.

Lesson 63

PART A   Word Lists

1
Mr. Taylor
hoarse
emotion
afford

2
Vocabulary words
1. down
2. receiver

3
Vocabulary words
1. wild goose chase
2. cast
3. hoarse
4. face
5. unexpectedly
6. fumble
7. sprawling

PART B   Main Idea Passages

Write the main idea sentence for each of the passages.
1. Oz promised the Tin Woodman that he would give him a heart.
   Oz promised the Scarecrow that he would give him brains.
   Oz promised the cowardly Lion that he would give him courage.

2. The dcsk in his house was dusty.
   The table in his house was dusty.
   The rocking chair in his house was dusty.

3. Men have emotions.
   Women have emotions.
   Children have emotions.

4. Nellie could jump over the highest barriers.
   Nellie could jump over middle-sized barriers.
   Nellie could jump over the lowest barriers.

PART C   Story Items

5. How could Julie tell if Martha was on the trail of her father or on the trail of an animal?
6. When Julie realized where Martha was going, Julie had a dismal feeling.
   a. Where was Martha going?
   b. Julie had a dismal feeling about that place because _____.
      • dogs could not track there
      • dogs barked there
      • it was far away
7. As Julie tried to climb up the rocks, she fell.
   a. What part of her body did she hurt?
   b. What else was damaged by the fall?
   c. What did she have to do to make that thing work?
8. a. Did Martha follow the same path that Julie's father had taken?
   b. Where was Julie when she finally caught up to Martha?
9. At first, Martha _____ the trail of Julie's father.
      • was on   • had lost
10. Julie noticed something in the valley to the south.
    a. What did she see?
    b. How did she signal?
11. a. Julie kept searching for the trail because she was afraid that scent might _____.
    b. When the people approached, what name did one of them call out?
    c. Write the names of the three people in the party who approached Julie.
    d. At first, did they believe that Martha was actually on the trail of Julie's father?

12. Julie and the others were talking when Martha caught the scent of something.
  a. What was it?
  b. How did Julie know that it wasn't the scent of her father?
13. Did the two men start to believe that Martha had been on the trail of Julie's father?

PART D   Review Items

14. Use the words in the box to fill in the blanks or replace the underlined words.

misery	determination	tore
hardships	ridge	spring
soiled	intense	
kennel	miracle	

  a. The mouse shredded cloth into strips and lined her nest with them.
  b. They washed the _____ clothes.
  c. She had no home and had experienced many other _____.
  d. After her dog died, she felt great _____.
  e. She had a very strong desire to win the race.
  f. The horse had such _____ to escape that nobody could catch her.
  g. The dogs were kept in their _____.

PART E   Writing Assignment

Pretend you are Julie, and that you are trying to convince the other people that Martha is on the right trail.

Write at least **four** sentences that tell what you would say.

Lesson 64

PART A   Word Lists

1
Vocabulary words
1. wild goose chase
2. sprawling
3. hoarse
4. cast
5. unexpectedly
6. face
7. operate

2
Vocabulary words
1. intently
2. emotions

PART B   Main Idea Passages

Write the main idea sentence for each of the passages.
  1. Some hot air balloons can cross the Pacific Ocean.
     Some sailboats can cross the Pacific Ocean.
     Some airplanes can cross the Pacific Ocean.

  2. Angela liked to play baseball.
     Angela liked to play hockey.
     Angela liked to play basketball.

  3. Martha could track the scent of a rabbit.
     Martha could track the scent of birds.
     Martha could track the scent of people.

4. The redwoods in the park were beautiful.
The live oaks in the park were beautiful.
The pines in the park were beautiful.

PART C   Story Items

5. a. What scent had Martha picked up first when Mr. Whitebird and the others were present?
   b. They could tell that Martha was on the right scent when she
      • howled.
      • let out a sharp bark.
      • was quiet.
6. When Martha kept barking, somebody responded in the distance. Who was that?
      • Leader   • Julie's mother
      • Mr. Whitebird
7. What did Mr. Whitebird do to Mr. Owl's leg?
8. a. Who ran ahead of the others after Mr. Owl was found?
   b. Why?
9. When everybody was in the station wagon, Julie kissed Martha and said, "Oh, thank you so much." Then what did everybody do?
10. Once Martha delivered a very large litter.
   a. How many puppies were in it?
   b. Julie's father said something to the runt. What did he tell that runt?
11. a. Did Julie walk better after she was operated on?
   b. Did she walk without a limp after the operation?
12. Julie told the doctor, "You don't have to be born perfect to be outstanding at doing some things." Who taught Julie that rule?

PART D   Review Items

13. Here are some statements that characters in the story might have said. Write whether they would have made each statement at the beginning of the story or at the end of the story.
   a. Julie's father might have said, "We don't want any runts in our kennel."
   b. Julie's mother might have said, "I don't think Martha will ever be a very good hunting dog, but we'll let Julie keep her anyhow."
   c. Julie's father might have said, "I'll never give a runt away again."
   d. Julie might have said, "Martha is the best hunting dog in the world."
   e. Julie's mother might have said, "If we could keep only one dog, it would be Martha."
   f. Julie's father might have said, "Runts can grow up to be good hunters."
   g. Julie might have said, "Martha may not ever grow up to be a good hunting dog, but I love her anyhow."
14. **Use the words in the box to fill in the blanks or replace the underlined words.**

decisively	reappear	halt
reluctant	afford	miracle
sensitive		misery

   a. The dog looked across the field and waited for her lost puppy to <u>come back into sight.</u>
   b. Denice knew she had to get to school on time, so she ran _____ down the street.
   c. When the Parker family discovered their house had burned down, they were in _____ .
   d. The food was terrible and she was _____ to eat it.
   e. With her _____ nose, the hound could smell people from a long way off.

PART E   Writing Assignment

Pretend you are Julie's mother. Write a story of Julie and Martha in your own words.

Write at least **five** sentences.

Lesson 65

PART A   Word Lists

1
airedale
terrier
Negroes
biography

2
greyhound
bloodhound
basketball
football

3
Vocabulary words
1. emotions
2. intently

4
Vocabulary words
1. herding
2. biography

PART B   Story Items

1. You have been reading about dogs.
   a. Name two kinds of dogs that you read long stories about.
   b. Which dog can work for days without food?
   c. Which dog has a more sensitive nose?
2. Let's say you are walking across a field with a hound and a sled dog.
   a. Which dog would pick up the scent of a rabbit first?
   b. Would that dog obey your commands?
   c. Would the sled dog obey your commands?
3. People have developed many breeds of dogs.
   a. Which breed has great speed?
   b. Which breed is very brave?
   c. Which breed herds sheep very well?
   d. Which breed has a very sensitive nose?
   e. Which breed may be the smartest?
4. a. Which two breeds would people use for parents if they wanted dogs that were smart and brave?
   b. Which two breeds would people use for parents if they wanted dogs that were fast and good at herding?
   c. Which two breeds would people use for parents if they wanted dogs that had sensitive noses and were smart?

PART C   Review Items

5. Write which story each statement describes. Choose from **A Horse to Remember, The Cat that Walked by Himself, Dick Whittington, The Ugly Duckling, Buck, Brown Wolf,** or **Adventure on the Rocky Ridge.**
   a. The story took place in northern Canada.
   b. The main character in this story wanted to live in a cave.
   c. The main character in this story wanted to live with swans.
   d. This story took place in California.
   e. One character in this story jumped over fences.
   f. The characters in this story included the woman, the baby, and the cow.
   g. One of the characters in this story walked with a limp?
   h. This story began in a nest.
   i. This story took place in London a long time ago.
   j. This story took place in modern-day England.

6. Use the words in the box to fill in the blanks.

guilty	naked
determination	hoarse
unexpectedly	afford
came down	sensitive
misery	kennel

a. The girl wore her old shoes until she could _____ to buy new ones.

b. The cruel man spread _____ wherever he went.

c. Rosa's sore foot was very _____ to anything that touched it.

d. The dog's ears flattened back and his eyes showed his _____ to continue.

e. After Derek took the dogs for a walk, he put them back in the _____.

f. The old man's voice was rough and _____.

g. The dog startled her when it appeared _____.

PART D   Writing Assignment

What is your favorite breed of dog?

Write at least **four** sentences that explain your answer.

Lesson 66

PART A   Word Lists

1	2	3	4
Ebbets Field	Jackie Robinson	**Vocabulary words**	**Vocabulary words**
Brooklyn	athlete	1. biography	1. major leagues
entrance	Dodgers	2. herding	2. plant
resent	umpire		3. bold
Phillies	league		4. daring
			5. athlete

PART B   Story Items

1. You read about the game of baseball.
   a. When a team is not batting, how many of its players are in the field?
   b. Which player is right behind the batter?
   c. Who stands right behind the catcher?
   d. When a batter gets a hit, which base does the batter go to first?
   e. Which base must the batter cross in order to score a run?

2. a. Who was the first black man to play major league baseball?
   b. In what year did he first play in the major leagues?
   c. What was the name of the baseball team that he played for?

3. That team moved to another city.
   a. To which city did that team move?
   b. When the team was in Brooklyn, which ball park did it play in?
   c. Is that ball park still standing?

4. a. Where did the man telling the story work?
   b. That man had a great interest that made his days more interesting. What interest did he have?

5. a. Did the people in the stands cheer for Jackie Robinson on the first day that he played for the Dodgers?
   b. Was the person telling the story a great fan of Jackie Robinson's on that first day?
   c. Did Jackie Robinson play well on the first day?

d. Jackie Robinson did not play well when he felt that people were _____ him.

e. How do you think Jackie Robinson would play when people supported him?

PART C Review Items

6. People have developed many breeds of dogs.
  a. Which breed of dog may be the smartest?
  b. Which breed of dog is good at herding?
  c. Which breed of dog has a very sensitive nose?
  d. Which breed of dog has great speed?
  e. Which breed of dog is very brave?

7. Look at the row of pictures below.

A   B   C

  a. Write the letter of the picture that shows a place that would hold an animal's scent well.
  b. Write the letter of the picture that shows a place that would hold a scent, but not too well.
  c. Write the letter of the picture that shows a place that would hold a scent very poorly.

8. Look at the picture below.

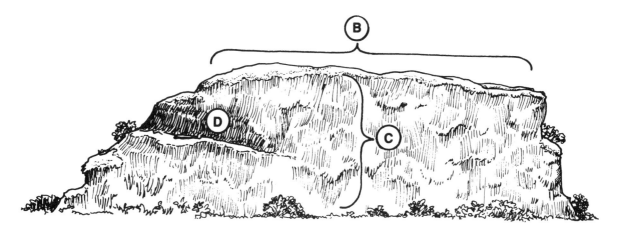

   a. Which letter shows a ledge?
   b. Which letter shows a ridge?
   c. Which letter shows the face?
9. Use the words in the box to fill in the blanks or replace the underlined words.

very dangerous	fumbled	misery
very strong	intently	reluctant
sprawling	miracle	emotions

   a. The heat from the furance was
      <u>intense</u>.
   b. Chan was eager to go skin diving, but
      at the last moment he became

      _____ .

   c. Olga _____ with the stack of
      books and then dropped them.
   d. The <u>spread out</u> oak tree shaded
      the whole lawn.
   e. She did not hear the thunder
      because she was reading her book
      <u>with concentration</u>.
   f. His <u>feelings</u> took over and he started
      to cry.

PART D   Writing Assignment

   Do you think that baseball is boring or
   interesting?

   Write at least **four** sentences that
   explain your answer.

Lesson 67

PART A   Word Lists

1
inspiration
appreciation
narrator

2
Pearl Harbor
Kansas City
Pittsburgh
Georgia
Hawaii
Honolulu
Germany
Missouri
Montreal
Kentucky

3
Branch Rickey
Eddie Stanky
lousy
fault
articles
addition
additional

4
Vocabulary words
1. bold
2. plant
3. daring
4. athlete

5
Vocabulary words
1. steal a base
2. National League Pennant
3. resent
4. dugout
5. talented
6. insult
7. appreciation
8. rookie
9. narrator

PART B   Story Items

1. a. Who was the general manager of the Dodgers?
   b. How did that man want to change baseball?
   c. Which black player did Rickey select to be the first in the majors?
   d. What did Robinson agree to do?
   e. What might have happened if Robinson had broken his agreement?
2. a. In what year did Jackie Robinson first play in the major leagues?
   b. Which team did he play for?
3. The narrator got into an argument at work.
   a. One person said, "When you're against one player, you're against _____."
   b. Which team did the Dodgers play that made the narrator start standing up for Jackie Robinson?
   c. What did the players on that team do to Robinson?
   d. What did Robinson do?
   e. What did the Dodger shortstop do to show that he was on Robinson's side?
4. a. How did Robinson start to play after that game?
   b. What did he know about his teammates?
   c. How did Robinson play when he felt people were on his side?
   d. What did Robinson like to do when he got on base?
5. a. What did the Dodgers win in 1947?
   b. Which player was most responsible for the team's success?
   c. Did the Dodgers win the World Series that year?
   d. What award did Jackie Robinson win that year?
      • best batter   • best fielder
      • Rookie of the Year
6. During which year did the narrator start to read about Jackie Robinson?

PART C   Review Items

7. Write where each story took place. Choose from **Canada, North Carolina, California,** or **England.**
   a. Adventure on the Rocky Ridge
   b. Dick Whittington
   c. Buck
   d. Brown Wolf

8. People have developed many breeds of dogs.
   a. Which breed has a very sensitive nose?
   b. Which breed is very brave?
   c. Which breed herds sheep?
   d. Which breed may be the smartest?

9. Use the words in the box to fill in the blanks or replace the underlined words.

determination	herding
put up with	hoarse
sprawling	intently
unexpectedly	halt
decisive	afford

   a. The man saved up his money until he could _____ to take a trip.
   b. The soldier always knew what to do and was very _____ about his actions.
   c. If you are stubborn and don't give up, you have great _____.
   d. Terry surprised him when he appeared _____.
   e. Katie was tired of seeing her dog spread out on her bed.
   f. They leaned forward and with concentration watched the movie.
   g. A collie is a good dog for rounding up sheep.

PART D   Writing Assignment

What do you think is harder, keeping quiet or fighting back?

Write at least **four** sentences that explain your answer.

Lesson 68

PART A   Word Lists

1	2	3	4
complain	college	**Vocabulary words**	**Vocabulary words**
conference	dribble	1. insult	1. run back a punt
Edgar	ping-pong	2. rookie	2. long jump
mechanic	professional	3. appreciation	3. complain
Olympic		4. resent	4. quarterback
schedule		5. talented	5. mechanic
fury			6. fury
			7. schedule

PART B   Story Items

1. a. In what year did Jackie Robinson first play in the major leagues?
   b. What team did he play with?
   c. To what state did his family move when he was very young?
2. a. When Jackie was a teen-ager, what did he become a member of?
   b. Name one thing the boys in that group would do.
   c. How did Jackie's mother feel about what was happening to her son?
3. A mechanic told Jackie that he was behaving like a particular animal. Which animal?
4. One of Jackie's brothers set a junior college record in one sporting event. Which event?
   • long jump   • 100-meter dash
   • one mile relay   • high jump
5. When Jackie turned away from the gang, which activities did he take up?
6. a. How long does a student go to junior college?
   b. How long does a student go to a regular college?
   c. What kind of college did Jackie Robinson go to first?
7. a. List the four sports Jackie played.
   b. How well did he do in those sports?
8. One day Jackie had a problem because two sporting events were scheduled at the same time.
   a. Which event did he go to first?
   b. Whose record did he break at that event?
   c. Where did he go next?
9. a. Which regular college did Jackie Robinson go to after he finished junior college?
   b. What was one reason he wanted to go to that college?
   c. What happened to Frank shortly after Jackie entered that college?
10. a. Which sports did Jackie compete in at that college?
    b. Which was his poorest sport?
    c. Was there any hope back then that he would play in the major leagues?

PART C   Review Items

11. Name a use for each animal. Choose from **hunting, food,** or **carrying things.**
    a. pig
    b. cat
    c. mule
    d. hound
    e. camel
12. **Use the words in the box to fill in the blanks or replace the underlined words.**

sensitive	herded	hoarse
athlete	daring	feeling
fumbled	spring	halt
intense	tore	

    a. The smell of onions was so <u>very strong</u> that it made her eyes water.
    b. Denise had a _____ ear and could hear someone coming in the distance.
    c. Parrots talk in a _____ screechy voice.
    d. It looked as if he had caught the ball, but then he _____ it.
    e. Marta was delighted, but her mother was not experiencing the same <u>emotion</u>.
    f. The sheep tried to run out of the field, but the dog _____ them back in.
    g. The _____ had won many awards in different sports.
    h. Phil stood on the edge of the cliff and plunged into the river with one _____ leap.

PART D   Writing Assignment

Do you think it is right to join a gang?

Write at least **four** sentences that explain your answer.

Lesson 69

PART A   Word Lists

1
decent
promote
accuse
graduated
career
Monarchs
Rae

2
strict
restrict
Japanese
practice
sizzle
organize
organization

3
Vocabulary words
1. fury
2. complain
3. schedule
4. mechanic

4
Vocabulary words
1. accused of
2. promoted
3. officer
4. graduate
5. scout
6. organization

5
Vocabulary words
1. restricted to
2. decent
3. career
4. rattled

PART B
Vocabulary Sentences

1. The hotels were restricted to white people, so no black people could go in them.
2. Jobs were so hard to find that he couldn't find a decent job.
3. He was so interested in working as a coach that he decided to make coaching his career.
4. The pitcher became so rattled that he couldn't even hold the ball.

PART C   Main Idea Passages

Write the main idea sentence for each of the passages.

1. The diamonds were very valuable.
   The rubies were very valuable.
   The emeralds were very valuable.

2. Joe picked up his toothbrush.
   Joe moved the toothbrush around in his mouth.
   Joe put his toothbrush away.

3. Buck could pull a very heavy sled.
   Buck could pull a very light sled.
   Buck could pull a sled that was frozen in ice.

4. Wild tigers live in the jungle.
   Wild zebras live in the jungle.
   Wild elephants live in the jungle.

PART D   Story Items

5. a. Which one of Jackie's brothers had been a very famous athlete?
   b. What kind of jobs did his brother have two years later?
   c. What did Jackie's mother have to do while Jackie was in college?

6. In 1941, what kind of league could black players play in?
7. a. What city did Jackie go to after he quit college?
      • Montreal   • Hawaii
      • Brooklyn   • Los Angeles
   b. What did Jackie do during the week?
   c. What did Jackie do on the weekends?
8. a. What war did the United States join in 1941?
   b. What did Jackie join within a couple of months?
   c. Within two years, Jackie became
      _____.
      • a private   • an officer
      • a pilot
9. a. The men in Jackie's outfit complained that they had to wait many hours to get a seat in a
      _____.
   b. When Jackie told the officer in charge of the camp about that problem, some of the officers said that Jackie was _____.
10. a. Another football team would not play the Army football team. Why?
    b. So what did Jackie refuse to do?

11. In 1944, Jackie played with a black professional baseball team.
   a. What was the name of that team?
   b. How much money did Jackie earn?
   c. Where did the members of the team often have to sleep when they went to different cities?
   d. Why did they have to sleep there?
   e. Where did they sometimes have to eat?
   f. Why did they have to eat there?
12. One of the scouts from the Brooklyn Dodgers told Jackie that the general manager of the Dodgers was thinking of starting up a new league.
   a. What kind of league?
   b. Which man was the head of the Brooklyn organization?
   c. Was he really looking for a lot of players to start a Negro league?
13. a. Which team in the Brooklyn organization was Jackie to start out with?
   b. Is that a major league team or a minor league team?
14. What did Rickey make Jackie Robinson promise?

PART E   Review Items

15. Use the words in the box to fill in the blanks.

unexpectedly	emotions
appreciation	insulted
reluctant	grapple
talented	reappear
athlete	resented

   a. Why is she always so shy and _____ to talk to people?
   b. As he stepped on to the bridge, it suddenly and _____ fell into the river.
   c. Although she was the strongest runner, she was not the best _____ in the group.
   d. Anita was angry and _____ the way they treated her.
   e. Nobody was as good at animal training as that _____ young man.
   f. After they had _____ her many times, she got very angry and left.
   g. Leroy wrote them a letter to show his _____ for the gift they sent.

PART F   Writing Assignment

Branch Rickey told Jackie Robinson how hard it would be for Jackie to be the first black player in the major leagues.

Write what you think Rickey said. Write at least **four** sentences.

Lesson 70

PART A   Word Lists

1	2	3	4
Poseidon	lease	**Vocabulary words**	**Vocabulary words**
Zeus	release	1. accused of	1. contract
Hermes	field	2. restricted to	2. cousin
Apollo	fielding	3. organization	3. balk
apologize		4. graduate	
balk		5. promoted	
cousin		6. officer	
honor		7. rattled	
		8. decent	
		9. career	

PART B   Story Items

1. a. Did Branch Rickey think that Robinson would have an easy time in Montreal?
   b. How did Rickey think the other players would treat Robinson at first?

2. a. Rickey told Robinson that he would need somebody from then on. Who was that somebody?
   b. What did Rickey say that Robinson and Rae should do?

3. Did anybody sit with Rae in the stands?

4. One day on the field, a player helped Jackie out.
   a. What position did that player play?
   b. What position was Jackie playing?

5. In the first game after spring practice, a lot of people came to watch Jackie.
   a. The second time Jackie was up to bat, he did something that thrilled the crowd. What did he do?
   b. The next time he was up to bat, he got a hit. How many bases did he steal?

6. a. What did the players of one team throw out on the field one day?
   b. What did Jackie use to answer them?
      • his bat   • his glove
      • his manager
   c. What did Jackie tell the players on the other team as he went past their dugout?

7. a. At the end of the season, what did Jackie's team win?
      • the World Series
      • the league pennant
      • second place
   b. What record did Jackie have?
      • top fielder   • top runner
      • top batter

PART C   Review Items

8. a. Which metal was discovered near Dawson in 1896?
   b. Which country is Dawson in?
   c. Which river flows through Dawson?
   d. Which story took place near Dawson?
   e. Who was the main character of that story?

9. Write **true** or **false** for each item.
   a. When you climb a mountain, it is like going south.
   b. Redwoods are shorter than oaks.
   c. California is one of the largest states.
   d. The tops of tall mountains are covered with snow.
   e. Brown Wolf decided to stay in California.

10. Write **fact** or **fiction** for each item.

    a. A newspaper story about a robbery

    b. A short story about a talking horse

    c. An encyclopedia article about horses

    d. A novel about a girl from Kansas

    e. An article about how to make shoes

11. Use the words in the box to fill in the blanks or replace the underlined words.

complained	resent
organization	rookie
mechanic	daring
intently	plod
emotions	soiled

    a. The cat crouched and <u>with concentration</u> watched the mice.

    b. The children's <u>feelings</u> took over and they started to cry.

    c. They risked their lives by doing many _____ things.

    d. At first he liked Joe, but after a time he began to <u>be angered by</u> Joe's bad habits.

    e. There was one <u>ball player in his first year</u> on the team.

    f. They took their car to the _____ to get it fixed.

    g. He _____ that the movie was very boring.

PART D   Writing Assignment

Pretend you are a newspaper reporter, who is writing an article about the first game that Jackie Robinson played after spring training.

Write at least **four** sentences.

Lesson 71

PART A   Word Lists

1
mlraculous
hospitality
honey
olive

2
Hcrmes
Poseidon
Apollo
Zeus

3
Vocabulary words
1. balk
2. contract
3. cousin

4
Vocabulary words
1. oppose
2. honor
3. bunt
4. retire
5. defeat

PART B   Main Idea Passages

Write the main idea sentence for each of the passages.

    1. Trucks use the freeway.
    Cars use the freeway.
    Buses use the freeway.

    2. Hubert put on his pants.
    Hubert put on his shirt.
    Hubert put on his shoes and socks.

    3. Francesca sat on her bike.
    Francesca turned the pedals.
    Francesca went down the street.

    4. People love to watch baseball.
    People love to watch hockey.
    People love to watch football.

PART C   Story Items

5. a. Where did the Montreal team go to play the minor league championship games?

   b. How well did Jackie do in those games?

   c. How many of the first three games did Montreal win?

   d. In which city were the next games played?

   e. How well did Jackie do in those games?

   f. Which team finally won the series?

   g. Who scored the winning run of the last game?

6. The next year was 1947. Who did Jackie play for that year?

7. Jackie won a lot of honors during the years he played. Write **two** of those honors.

8. Jackie didn't play every game during the 1955 season. What were people saying about him?

9. Jackie played in the third game of the 1955 World Series.

   a. Who usually won the World Series when the Dodgers and the Yankees played?

   b. Who won the Series in 1955?

   c. Who was the star of the Series?

10. In what year did Jackie retire from baseball?

11. One sports writer wrote of Jackie Robinson: "He would not be defeated, not by the other team and not by _____."

PART D   Review Items

12. Write what each character wanted from Oz.

   a. Scarecrow

   b. Lion

   c. Dorothy

   d. Tin Woodman

13. Use the words in the box to fill in the blanks or replace the underlined words.

promoted	terrible	fury
accused of	mechanic	lean
scheduled	business	feeling
unexpectedly	talented	graduate

   a. The dog growled at Anton _____ and surprised him.

   b. Marta was delighted but Olga did not experience the same <u>emotion</u>.

   c. Lucy was a very good _____ and could repair any machine.

   d. Hank was a good writer and had always been _____ with words.

   e. The bears growled and fought because they were full of <u>great anger</u>.

   f. The movie started at 3:30 and she _____ her time so that she would not be late.

   g. Deborah was _____ a crime she had not committed.

   h. The company was a very large <u>organization</u>.

   i. Ann will _____ from high school in three months.

   j. Gina was not happy with her job and wanted to be _____ to a better one.

PART E   Writing Assignment

Pretend you are a Brooklyn Dodger fan who had watched Jackie Robinson play from 1947 through 1956. You have just found out that Jackie is retiring from baseball. Write a letter to Jackie and tell Jackie what he meant to you.

Write at least **four** sentences.

Lesson 72

PART A Word Lists

1	2	3	4	5
Philemon	beehive	lodge	**Vocabulary words**	**Vocabulary words**
Baucis	grapevine	lodging	1. honor	1. miraculous
cultivate	neighborhood	vegetable	2. retire	2. hospitality
fertile	nightfall	disagreeable	3. defeat	3. cultivate
	mudball	lightfooted	4. oppose	4. fertile
		youth		5. staff
		fragrant		6. toiled

PART B Main Idea Paragraphs

Read each paragraph below. For each paragraph, figure out who the main character is and what main thing that character did. Then write a sentence that tells the main idea. Start by naming the main character, then tell **what** the character did. You can write **when** the character did it, **where** the character did it, or **why** or **how** the character did it.

1.   It was a week before Christmas, and Clara had purchased presents for everyone in her family except for her brother, Tony. She knew some of the things that Tony wanted, but most of them were far too expensive for Clara to buy. So, Clara went to the department store without knowing exactly what she would buy. She looked at clothing. She looked at sporting equipment. Then, as she was walking by the tool department, she recalled that her brother spent a lot of time fixing his bike. But he never seemed to have the right tool. So, Clara inquired about a tool kit for fixing bikes. The clerk showed her a nice bike-repair tool kit that was not too expensive. Clara said, "I'll take it."

2.   It was time for lunch. Sidney followed the other students into the lunchroom. But Sidney was not hungry, so he sat at one of the tables. Then he took a paper and pencil and began to write. He stopped and thought for a moment. Then he wrote some more. Soon, Sidney was finished. Here is what he wrote:

> The lunchroom has a lot to eat;
> Milk, and bread, and cheese, and
>   meat.
> But on this day I would rather think,
> Than get some things to eat and
>   drink.

PART C Story Items

3. Baucis and Philemon lived in a cottage.
   a. Were they young or old?
   b. Were they rich or poor?
   c. Were their dinners large or small?
   d. Who would they treat better, themselves or their guests?
4. Their cottage was near a valley.
   a. What had the valley been long ago?
   b. What had people built in the valley after the water dried up?
   c. Was the village attractive or unattractive?
5. a. The people who lived in the village were _____.
   • kind   • mean   • unselfish
   b. What would their children do to strangers?
   c. What else would attack strangers?

6. a. Baucis and Philemon were having trouble carrying on a conversation because _____.
- the villagers made noise
- they did not hear well
- the lake made noise

b. The noise told them that _____ had come to the village.

c. The noise was coming toward the _____.

7. a. How many travelers approached their cottage?

b. Did they look poor or rich?

c. Why did Baucis go into the cottage?

d. What did Philemon do while Baucis went inside?

8. The younger traveler was dressed in an odd way.

a. What did he have in his hand?

b. What unusual things were on the staff?

9. Tell which character each statement describes. Choose from **Philemon,** the **younger traveler,** or from a **village child.**

a. This character has strange shoes.

b. This character would give his food to a stranger.

c. This character would laugh at strangers and do mean things.

d. This character would throw stones at strangers.

e. This character would do anything for a guest.

f. This character was in good spirits.

g. This character worked in his garden all day long.

h. This character's feet seemed to rise from the ground.

i. This character would not give any food to a stranger.

PART D   Review Items

10. Use the words in the box to fill in the blanks or replace the underlined words.

restricted to	career	intently
appreciation	accuse	plod
insulting	talent	complain
scheduled	fumble	resented
contract		

a. Clara's aunt did many things for her, but Clara never showed much _____.

b. They _____ dinner for 9:00 in the evening.

c. They did not have enough facts to _____ the man of stealing the jewels.

d. Norma watched Howard's face with concentration to see if he was lying.

e. The music was very loud and she was angered by the noise it made.

f. To be a great pianist, you have to have a great deal of _____.

g. Bruce did not leave, even though the others kept _____ him.

h. Luis didn't want to work for the circus until he had a _____ with the owners.

i. The playground was _____ children younger than ten years old.

j. Rachel worked in a shoe store but didn't want to make a main job of selling shoes.

PART E   Writing Assignment

Which god do you think the younger stranger is?

Write at least **three** sentences that explain your answer.

Lesson 73

PART A   Word Lists

1	2	3	4	5
sympathy	carelessly	**Vocabulary words**	**Vocabulary words**	**Vocabulary words**
disguise	suddenly	1. fertile	1. shrewd and witty	Poseidon
shrewd	continually	2. miraculous	2. in disguise	Hermes
Quicksilver	sorrowfully	3. staff	3. sympathy	Zeus
gesture	eagerly	4. hospitality	4. nimble	Apollo
		5. cultivate		
		6. toiled		

PART B   Main Idea Paragraphs

Read each paragraph below. For each paragraph, figure out who the main character is and what main thing that character did. Then write a sentence that tells the main idea. Start by naming the main character, then tell **what** the character did. You can write **when** the character did it, **where** the character did it, or **why** or **how** the character did it.

1.   Rochelle thought that March would never come. January and February were very cold and long, and the city park was covered with snow. But at last, March came and all the snow in the park melted. Rochelle went to her closet and got out the kite she had made last year. Then she tied some string to the kite and went to the park. She held the string in her hand and started to run. The kite went into the air. Rochelle stopped running and started to let out more string. She watched the kite dart back and forth in the sky. After several hours, she pulled the kite back in and walked home.

2.   Veronica liked to watch birds from her bedroom window. The birds spent a lot of time sitting on the telephone pole in the alley behind her house. But Veronica wanted the birds to sit closer to her window. So, last weekend, she went to the lumber yard and bought several pieces of wood. She nailed some of the pieces together to make a box. Then she put a roof on the box and cut a hole in one side to make a door. She filled the box with birdseed. Then she hung the box right outside her window. Soon, the birds came to the place that Veronica had built.

PART C   Story Items

3. Philemon talked to the older stranger about the village.
   a. What did the stranger say had once been where the village stands?
   b. What happened to the twilight when the stranger frowned?
   c. Did Philemon think the older stranger was wise or stupid?

4. a. Had Philemon ever seen the lake?
   b. What was the farthest distance Philemon had ever been from his cottage?
   c. What kind of food did Philemon raise in his garden?
   d. Who did Philemon want to be with him after he died?

5. a. Why was Baucis so worried when everyone went into the cottage to eat supper?

  b. What was there to drink?

  c. Write the names of **two** other foods that were on the table.

6. a. How did Quicksilver's staff get into the cottage?

  b. What part of the staff made it move?

  c. Did Baucis and Philemon see the staff move?

7. a. After Baucis gave the strangers milk from the pitcher, how much milk was left in the pitcher?

  b. After the strangers drank their milk, how many more cups of milk did Quicksilver pour out of the pitcher?

  c. Quicksilver was always _____.
   ● smiling   ● frowning
   ● shouting

PART D   Review Items

8. Use the words in the box to fill in the blanks or replace the underlined words.

complained	defeated	oppose
graduated	emotions	resented
talented	careers	contract
business	mechanic	

  a. They cheated him and he <u>was angry at</u> them for that.

  b. Although she wasn't very _____, she eventually learned to sing well.

  c. Margie was often sick, but she never _____ about the way she felt.

  d. When the students had finished their last year of school, they _____.

  e. Lana was president of an important <u>organization</u>.

  f. Before they signed the _____, they read it carefully.

  g. When he changed _____, he quit one job and started another.

  h. The mayor presented a plan but most of the people said that they would <u>be against</u> it.

  i. No one liked to play against her because she could not be <u>beaten</u>.

PART E   Writing Assignment

Which god do you think the older stranger is?

Write at least **three** sentences that explain your answer.

Lesson 74

PART A   Word Lists

1
fragrance
century
abundant
spacious
inhabitant

2
Vocabulary words
1. in disguise
2. shrewd and witty
3. nimble
4. sympathy

3
Vocabulary words
1. astonishment
2. inhabitant
3. disagreeable
4. spacious
5. abundant
6. century
7. fragrance

PART B   Main Idea Paragraphs

Read each paragraph below. For each paragraph, figure out who the main characters are and what main thing those characters did. Then write a sentence that tells the main idea. Start by naming the main characters, then tell **what** the characters did. You can write **when** the characters did it, **where** the characters did it, or **why** or **how** the characters did it.

1.   It was the Fourth of July. Mr. and Mrs. Dunbar woke up early and began to prepare for the day's big event. Mr. Dunbar made chicken sandwiches and a big potato salad. He put the sandwiches and salad in a large basket, then went to his children's bedrooms to wake them up. Meanwhile, Mrs. Dunbar put gas in the car and checked the oil and tires. Then she picked up the family and the food and drove to Red Rock State Park. When they got to the park, the Dunbars got out of the car and put some blankets on the ground. Then they ate all the food, played volleyball, and went on a hike. They stayed at Red Rock State Park until sunset.

2.   The Comets were one of the best softball teams in Springfield. There were five girls and five boys on the team, and they won almost all their games. By September, the Comets had won so many games that they ended up playing in the City Championship game. The Comets were certain that they would win. At the end of three innings, they had a five run lead. But the other team started to come back. By the last inning, the Comets were one run behind the other team. The Comets had only one more chance to bat. But the Comets did not score a run in that inning. The Comets were brokenhearted, but they went over to congratulate the other team.

PART C   Story Items

3. a. Who do you think Quicksilver is?
   b. Who do you think the older traveler is?
4. Quicksilver asked Baucis for some more milk.
   a. Did Baucis think that there was any milk left in the pitcher?
   b. Why was Baucis so surprised when she tilted the pitcher?
   c. When the strangers held the grapes, the grapes became _____ .
5. a. When Baucis told Philemon about the pitcher, did he believe her?
   b. What did Philemon see forming at the bottom of the pitcher?
   c. Quicksilver said that an object had charmed the pitcher. Which object was that?
6. a. Where did Baucis and Philemon sleep that night?
   b. Who occupied their bed?
7. a. Why did Baucis want to go to the village later that day?
   b. What did Quicksilver say that he couldn't see?

PART D   Review Items

8. Use the words in the box to fill in the blanks or replace the underlined words.

great anger	intense
restricted to	fertile
hospitality	oppose
appreciation	accused
miraculous	wrestle
promoted	herding
cultivated	

a. Willie showed his _____ of the meal by eating three servings.

b. The wildcat screamed with <u>fury</u> at the hunter and his dogs.

c. The teacher _____ his students of throwing papers in the hall.

d. If Nathan did better work at his job, he would be _____.

e. The swimming pool was _____ adults, and children were not allowed.

f. He was so angry that he decided to be <u>against</u> the decision.

g. They could not believe the <u>miracle-like</u> things the magician could do.

h. When visiting with her cousins, Rita was grateful for their <u>kindness</u>.

i. They could make no money from their farm because the land was not <u>capable of growing very good crops.</u>

j. The field had not been _____ and it was full of weeds.

PART E   Writing Assignment

Do you know anybody like Baucis and Philemon?

Write at least **four** sentences that explain your answer.

Lesson 75

PART A   Word Lists

1
sour
calculate
inhale

2
fertile
hospitality
pause
circular

3
Vocabulary words
1. inhabitant
2. spacious
3. abundant
4. disagreeable
5. century
6. astonishment

4
Vocabulary words
1. inhale
2. calculate
3. sift
4. gleam

PART B
Vocabulary Sentences

1. He was out of breath and was breathing very hard—first breathing out, then <u>inhaling</u>.

2. He was always figuring things out. So when he looked at the gifts, he <u>calculated</u> what they must cost.

3. The little girl poured sand into her hand and watched it <u>sift</u> through her fingers.

4. The bowl was so bright and shiny that it <u>gleamed</u> in the sunlight.

PART C Main Idea Paragraphs

Read each paragraph below. For each paragraph write a sentence that tells the main idea.

1.   Last summer, the Chavez family got on the train in Los Angeles. The train pulled out of the Los Angeles station and started heading east. The Chavez family looked out the window at the passing scenery. They saw the city, then saw some mountains, then some deserts, then some more mountains. The train stopped in Denver, Colorado. The Chavez family spent the next day watching the prairie. That night, the train pulled into Chicago. But the Chavez family did not get off. After a while, the train left Chicago and passed by many farms and small towns. After one more night, the train finally arrived in New York City. The Chavez family got off the train and walked into the New York train station.

2.   It was springtime, and all the people around Liverpool were talking about the steeplechase that was coming up. People talked about all the different horses, but almost nobody talked about Chico. Chico was a brown horse with white spots. On the day of the steeplechase, Chico lined up with all the other horses and waited for the signal to start. The signal went off, and all the horses started running. Chico was far behind at first, but as the race continued, he came closer and closer to the lead. At the last jump, Chico took the lead, and was the first horse to cross the finish line.

PART D Story Items

3. a. What happened to the village on the morning the strangers departed?
   b. Who do you think changed the valley into a lake?
   c. Write the names of the two people who were worried about the villagers.
   d. What had the villagers been changed into?
   e. Why were the villagers like those animals?
4. a. What did Baucis and Philemon say they most wanted in the world?
   b. What happened to their cottage?
5. a. What happened to the strangers when Philemon and Baucis got on their knees to thank them?
   b. What did Baucis and Philemon do in the palace?
   c. How did milk from the pitcher taste to friendly guests?
   d. How did milk from the pitcher taste to disagreeable guests?
6. a. When Baucis and Philemon disappeared, what were they changed into?
   b. Where were those two objects?
   c. What names did the trees seem to murmur?
   d. What did somebody build around the trees?
   e. What kind of people would sit there?
   f. What would they drink when they sat there?
   g. Where would that liquid come from?

PART E Review Items

7. Write **true** or **false** for each statement.
   a. Gold was discovered in Juneau in 1896.
   b. When you climb a mountain, it is like going south.
   c. Mount Whitney is the highest mountain in California.
   d. Redwoods are very short trees.
   e. The Yukon River flows through Dawson.
   f. California is the largest state.

8. Use the words in the box to fill in the blanks or replace the underlined words.

shrewd and witty	beat	accused
miraculous	resent	cultivate
sympathy	career	oppose
appreciation	nimble	

a. Her mother _____ her of lying.

b. They bowed and thanked him with sincere _____ for the fine things he did.

c. Keith loved his work because his <u>main job</u> was very important to him.

d. Natalie tried to outrun Janice but could not <u>defeat</u> her.

e. The farmers worked hard to _____ the field.

f. When they came out of the cave, they saw a <u>miracle-like</u> sight.

g. Everyone felt _____ for the poor beggar.

h. They laughed at the <u>smart and funny</u> things he said.

i. Jill was so _____ that she could walk on eggs without breaking them.

PART F   Writing Assignment

In the story, Baucis and Philemon were changed into trees. Compare Baucis and Philemon with trees. Tell how they are the same, and how they are different.

Write at least **four** sentences.

Lesson 76

PART A   Word Lists

1	2	3	4
Midas	Marygold	petal	**Vocabulary words**
pooh	buttercup	fragrant	1. calculate
chink	farewell	conclude	2. gleam
	bedside	perfume	3. sift
	handrail	concluded	4. inhale
	staircase		
	hallway		

PART B   Main Idea Paragraphs

Read each paragraph below. Then write a sentence that tells the main idea.

1.   Saturday finally arrived, and Janet took her camera out of her closet. Then she went outside to look for her friends. She found Hector and Lynn right away, but it took her almost half an hour to get everybody else. When she had found everybody, she told them to stand together on her porch. She looked through her camera at her friends, then told them to stand closer together. Finally, she said, "Smile," and pressed the button on the camera. The camera went "click" and some of Janet's friends made faces.

2.   William liked rowing boats. In 1975, William visited Swan Lake. He saw a boat rental place, and rented a rowboat for the whole day. He hopped into the boat and started to pull on the oars. The boat started across the lake. William could see the boat rental place getting farther and farther away. William kept rowing. He looked at people fishing and at birds flying near the water. He had fun seeing how fast he could row. After a long time, William came to the opposite side of the lake.

PART C   Story Items

3. **a.** What did Midas love most of all?
   b. What did he love almost as much?
   c. But the more Midas loved
   _____ , the more he loved
   _____ .

4. Midas had not always had that desire for gold.
   a. What kind of flowers had he planted?
   b. What would Midas do with those flowers?
   c. What was the strange music Midas loved now?

5. **a.** Where did Midas keep his gold?
   b. How much time did he spend with his gold?
   c. How did Midas feel when he was looking at his gold?

6. Only one sunbeam came from the basement window. Why did Midas like that sunbeam?

7. **a.** Who appeared in the basement one day?
   b. What color was the glow of the stranger's smile?
   c. What happened to the gold in the room when the stranger smiled?
   d. What kind of person did Midas think the stranger was?
   e. Why was Midas surprised to find somebody in his room?
   f. What did Midas think the stranger might do for him?

PART D   Review Items

8. **Use the words in the box to fill in the blanks or replace the underlined word.**

fertile	restricted to
in disguise	oppose
graduate	hospitality
sympathy	resented

   a. Travelers liked the old couple because they offered their <u>kindness</u> to all.
   b. The party was _____ members of the club.
   c. He experienced many hardships, but no one showed him any _____ .
   d. It was good farmland because it was so _____ .
   e. They did not recognize her because she was _____ .

PART E   Writing Assignment

If the stranger is a god who can grant wishes, write what Midas might ask the stranger to do.

Write at least **three** sentences that explain your answer.

PART F   Special Projects

1. You have read about four Greek gods. There were many other Greek gods. Look in an encyclopedia or other reference books and try to find the names of all the gods who lived on Mount Olympus. Make a list of all those gods and tell what each god controlled. If you wish, you can also draw a picture of each god.

2. Make up a play based on The <u>Miraculous Pitcher</u>. Figure out what the characters will say. You can either use words from the story or make up your own words. Then decide who will play each character, and who will work on the costumes and scenery. Finally, put on the play for the whole class.

Lesson 77

PART A   Word Lists

1
linen
frenzy
appetite
credit
woven
dispair
pity
secure

2
precious
delicious
anxious
spacious

3
flexible
convenient
inconvenient
accompany
accompanied

4
Vocabulary words
1. deserve credit
2. linen
3. frenzy
4. occupied
5. envy
6. despair

5
Vocabulary words
1. discontent
2. appetite
3. secure
4. pity

PART B
Vocabulary Sentences

1. She was very unhappy about a lot of things, but she was most <u>discontented</u> about the mess that was in the basement.
2. When he started eating he had a huge <u>appetite</u>, but when he finished the main part of the meal, he had no room for dessert.
3. He didn't want anybody to steal his treasure, so he looked for a <u>secure</u> place.
4. The little boy was so poor, sad, and cold that I felt great <u>pity</u> for him.

PART C   Main Idea Paragraphs

Read the paragraph below. Then write a sentence that tells the main idea.

1.   Baucis and Philemon lived in a small cottage outside a village. They did not have much money or food, but they were happy. Sometimes, they would see a stranger walking up the path to their cottage. At those times, Baucis would hurry into the house to make dinner and Philemon would greet the stranger. Then Baucis and Philemon would give the stranger some dinner and do everything they could to make the stranger comfortable. After dinner, they would give up their bed to the stranger and sleep on the floor.

PART D   Story Items

2. **a.** Before the stranger came to his room, was Midas satisfied with the wealth he had?
   b. Why didn't Midas just ask for a mountain of gold?
   c. What did Midas ask the stranger for?
   d. Did Midas think he would ever regret that gift?
3. Midas woke up early the next morning.
   a. Did the golden touch work at first?
   b. When did the golden touch begin to work?
   c. What was the first object that changed into gold?
   d. After Midas touched the book, what couldn't he do with that book?
4. **a.** When Midas put on his clothes, what was different about their weight?
   b. Write the name of the first object that disturbed Midas when it changed to gold.
   c. Who had made that object for Midas?
5. **a.** What kind of flowers did Midas touch?
   b. How did the flowers smell before he touched them?
   c. How did they smell after he touched them?

PART E   Review Items

6. Write which breed of dog each statement describes.
   a. This is the fastest breed.
   b. This breed is good at herding.
   c. This breed has an excellent nose.
   d. This may be the smartest breed.
   e. This breed is very brave.

7. Write which character could have made each statement. Choose from the **Lion,** the **Cat that Walked,** or the **Ugly Duckling.**
   a. "I am the king of beasts."
   b. "I live with people, but they can't tell me what to do."
   c. "I used to be a coward."
   d. "I finally saw myself when I looked in the water."
   e. "I saw how the woman fooled all the other animals."

8. Use the words in the box to fill in the blanks or replace the underlined words.

disagreeable	insulted	rookie
astonishment	contract	beat
main job	a lot of	spacious
in disguise	inhabitants	

   a. The rainy weather was very _____ to Sidney.
   b. Cora decided to go to a school that would prepare her for a new career.
   c. She didn't want to perform in the play, but she had a _____ that said she had to.
   d. At the Halloween party, Mary was _____ as a bear.
   e. They were surprised and full of amazement.
   f. Most of the _____ of the town chased the frogs into the lake.
   g. Their footsteps echoed in the _____ halls.
   h. They loaded their sled with abundant supplies.

PART F   Writing Assignment

Write at least **four** sentences about the problems you might have if you had the golden touch.

Lesson 78

PART A   Word Lists

1	2	3
occupy	coffee	**Vocabulary words**
ornaments	experiment	1. deserve credit
terrify	breakfast	2. pity
	potato	3. secure
	appearance	4. discontented
	woven	5. envy
		6. appetite
		7. occupied
		8. linen
		9. frenzy
		10. despair

PART B   Main Idea Paragraphs

Read the paragraph below. Then write a sentence that tells the main idea.

1.   School was out, and Hopkinsville seemed like the most boring town on earth. Frank liked the month of June, but he did not like Hopkinsville. There was almost nothing to do. But there were a lot of things going on in Center City, which was a town about ten miles from Hopkinsville. Frank was too young to drive, and his bike had a flat tire, so he set out for Center City on foot. Frank enjoyed walking, and stopped often to look at farmers working in their fields. He crossed the river shortly before coming into Center City. Finally, three hours after he had started, Frank arrived in the city.

PART C   Story Items

2. a. Write the names of **three** foods that were served to Midas for breakfast.
   b. Why did Midas wait to begin his breakfast?
   c. Why did Marygold's crying surprise Midas?
   d. Why was Marygold so unhappy?
   e. Who had changed the roses?
3. a. Why couldn't Midas drink the coffee?
   b. Why would Midas rather have had a real fish instead of a gold one?
   c. What food did Midas try to eat very quickly?
   d. What did that food do to his mouth?
4. a. Was Midas' breakfast worth a lot of money?
   b. Could Midas eat the breakfast?
   c. Tell why.
5. a. Who ran toward Midas?
   b. At that moment, what did Midas feel was worth more, his daughter's love, or the golden touch?
   c. Did Marygold speak after Midas kissed her?
   d. Tell why.

6. When common objects are changed into gold, they may be worth more money, but they may not be as useful.
   a. When spectacles are changed, you can't _____ through them.
   b. When roses are changed, you can't _____ them.
   c. When a fish is changed, you can't _____ it.
   d. When coffee is changed, you can't _____ it.
7. After breakfast, what did Midas think was worth more, gold or a piece of bread?

PART D   Review Items

8. **Use the words in the box to fill in the blanks or replace the underlined words.**

astonishment	sympathy	rookie
restricted to	century	fury
breathe in	gleamed	nimble
calculate	promote	

   a. The playground was _____ students from Spring Lake School.
   b. Adam's fingers were fast and <u>not awkward</u>.
   c. The people were suffering but the king showed very little _____ for them.
   d. The old man had lived for almost a _____.
   e. The children were filled with <u>amazement</u> as they watched the clown's tricks.
   f. She paused to <u>inhale</u> the fragrance of the roses.
   g. They tried to <u>figure out</u> how much water was in the bathtub.
   h. The jewels glittered and _____.

PART E   Writing Assignment

Do you think Midas regrets asking for the golden touch?

Write at least **four** sentences that explain your answer.

Lesson 79

PART A   Word Lists

1	2	3	4
original	deadly	teardrops	**Vocabulary words**
victim	faithfully	wring	1. insane
desolate	seriously	moisten	2. dimple
	sincerely	stretched	3. greedy
	immediately	outstretched	4. vanish
	instantly	terrify	5. glossy
		county	6. original
		country	7. victim
		countries	

PART B   Main Idea Paragraphs

Read the paragraph below. Then write a
sentence that tells the main idea.

1.   The year was 1896. A boat with
three men in it floated down the
Klondike River. At one point, the boat
stopped and the men got out. They had
seen something at the bottom of the
river. One of the men scooped up a
handful of dirt and pebbles from the
bottom of the river. He sifted through
the material and saw something that
glistened yellow in the sun. He looked
more closely, then let out a whoop of
joy. "We're going to be rich," he said.
The other men began to scoop up the
pebbles as fast as they could.

PART C   Story Items

2. **a.** Marygold had been changed into a
golden _____.
   b. Was her flesh soft, or hard?
3. **a.** Who told Midas how to get rid of the
golden touch?
   b. To rid himself of the golden touch,
Midas had to _____.
   • jump into a rose bush
   • jump into the river
   • drink milk
   c. What did Midas have to do to change
objects back to normal?
4. **a.** When Midas ran to the river, why
did his trail look like autumn?

b. What material did the vase change
back to?
c. Why did Midas feel lighter when he
was in the water?
d. What was the first thing that Midas
sprinkled water over?
e. Did Marygold remember anything
about when she was a statue?
f. What things in the garden did Midas
change back to their original form?
5. **a.** What part of Marygold always
reminded Midas of the golden touch?
   b. How did Midas feel about the sight
of gold at the end of the story?
   c. When he was an old man, Midas
loved to tell the story of the golden
touch to _____.
6. Write which character each statement
describes. Choose from **Midas,
Marygold,** or **the stranger.**
   a. This character was a god.
   b. This character learned a lesson.
   c. This character could not eat
breakfast.
   d. This character picked roses for her
father.
   e. This character was the main
character.
   f. This character had golden hair.
   g. This character's smile made objects
glow.
   h. This character plunged into the
river.
7. Complete the moral of The Golden
Touch. _____ is better than
_____ .

PART D   Review Items

8. When common objects are changed into gold, they may not be as useful.
   a. When roses are changed, you can't _____ them.
   b. When milk is changed, you can't _____ it.
   c. When a book is changed, you can't _____ it.
   d. When bread is changed, you can't _____ it.

9. **Use the words in the box to fill in the blanks or replace the underlined words.**

one hundred years	frenzy
appetite	envied
inhabitants	spacious
inhaled	occupied
disagreeable	contract
linen	career
nimble	

   a. Wayne agreed to do the things that were written in his _____.
   b. When Fred was in a bad mood, he was quite _____.
   c. The stunt woman was very _____.
   d. The cave was quiet and empty after the _____ had left.
   e. The big house had very _____ rooms.
   f. She breathed in deep gulps of air.
   g. When Margo realized that she was late, she began to move in a very hurried and excited way.
   h. The starving man was so busy with the thought of food that he couldn't think of anything else.
   i. She had never done well at sports and had always _____ people who did well.

PART E   Writing Assignment

Do you know anybody like Midas.

Write at least **four** sentences that explain your answer.

Lesson 80

PART A   Word Lists

1	2	3
soothe	shipwreck	ridicule
persuade	horseback	Beauty
pirates	anybody	cautious
poverty	halfway	fatigue
conceal	courtyard	excuses
dread		ridiculed
hasty		countries
		furniture

4
Vocabulary words
1. vanish
2. original
3. insane
4. glossy
5. dimple
6. greedy
7. victim

5
Vocabulary words
1. desolate
2. persuade
3. terrify
4. selfish
5. soothe
6. poverty

PART B
Vocabulary Sentences

1. There was nothing within a hundred miles of this lonely, desolate place.
2. She was very good at talking people into doing things, but she could not persuade anybody to go to the beach with her.
3. The old house was very frightening, and the sounds within that house terrified me.
4. She seemed to be very kind, but she was really very selfish and thought of nobody but herself.
5. He was so upset that nothing we could do would comfort and soothe him.
6. At first, he was wealthy, but then he lost all his wealth and found himself in poverty.

PART C   Main Idea Paragraphs

Read the paragraph below. Then write a sentence that tells the main idea.

1.   Joanne liked to listen to songs on the radio. Last Saturday, she heard a song that she really enjoyed. Joanne hurried off to the record store. The woman at the store had never heard of the song. She looked through all the recent records until she found a label with the song. Joanne paid the woman, then ran home to play the record on her record player.

PART D   Story Items

2. a. At the beginning of the story, how rich was the merchant?
   b. How many children did the merchant have?
   c. What happened to his house?
   d. What happened to his ships?
   e. What was the only thing he had left?
   f. How far from town was that thing?
3. a. Why were most of his children greedy and spoiled?
   b. Which child was not spoiled?
   c. Who was happier in the cottage, Beauty or her sisters?
4. a. What news made the children think that they would be rich again?
   b. Where did the merchant go?
   c. What did Beauty ask her father to bring back for her?
   d. What kinds of things did the other children ask for?
   e. What had the merchant's partners done with the goods from the ship?
   f. So was the merchant poorer or richer than when he left?
   g. What was the weather like when the merchant started to return home?
   h. Where did the merchant spend the night?

5. In the morning, the merchant came to a row of trees.
   a. What was strange about the ground around the trees?
   b. What kind of trees were they?
   c. What was at the end of the row of trees?
   d. Why was the palace so silent?
   e. What did the merchant find next to him when he woke up?
6. a. After the merchant ate, he went to
      _____.
      • the garden   • his cottage
      • the town
   b. What was the weather like in the garden?
   c. The merchant thought that all that magic had been created for _____.
   d. The merchant decided to share all that magic with _____.
   e. Why did the merchant stop to pick a rose?
   f. Who appeared when the merchant did that?
   g. What did the Beast threaten to do to the merchant?
7. Here are some events from this part of the story.
   a. Write the event that occurred **first**.
   b. Write the event that occurred **last**.
      • The merchant found a palace.
      • The merchant picked a rose for Beauty.
      • The merchant and his children moved to a cottage.
      • The merchant's house burned down.
      • The merchant went back to the town.

PART E   Review Items

8. Use the words in the box to fill in the blanks or replace the underlined words.

shrewd and witty	century
desire for food	safe
inhabitant	sympathy
discontented	shine
figure out	defeat

a. Lillian was so <u>dissatisfied</u> with her job that she quit.
b. The wise man made many _____ remarks.
c. A _____ is a long time.
d. The experts could not <u>calculate</u> the number of stars in the sky.
e. She was glad to see the food because she had an enormous <u>appetite</u>.
f. The cat was <u>secure</u> from dogs as long as it stayed inside the house.
g. After the child fell, her mother held her and showed great _____.

PART F   Writing Assignment

What do you think the Beast looks like?

Write at least **five** sentences that describe the Beast. You can also draw a picture of the Beast.

Lesson 81

PART A   Word Lists

1
permission
solution
condition
possession
mention

2
fault
curiosity
sensible

3
Vocabulary words
1. selfish
2. terrify
3. soothe
4. desolate
5. persuade
6. poverty

4
Vocabulary words
1. dread
2. hasty
3. conceal

PART B
Vocabulary Sentences

1. She hated the thought of leaving town, but she <u>dreaded</u> leaving her mother most of all.
2. They were in such a hurry that they ate a <u>hasty</u> breakfast.
3. She did not want the Beast to know that she was afraid, so she <u>concealed</u> her fear.

PART C   Main Idea Paragraph

Read the paragraph below. Then write a sentence that tells the main idea.

1.   Brown Wolf did not know what to do. Skiff Miller was walking away on the trail, and Brown Wolf was tempted to follow him. But the Irvines were staying in Glen Ellen, and Brown Wolf was also tempted to stay with them. The dog turned one way, and then the other. He tried to stop Skiff Miller, then he tried to make the Irvines follow Miller. After a few minutes, Brown Wolf got up and ran after the man who had raised him in the Klondike.

PART D　Story Items

2. The Beast said that he would let the merchant live on one condition.
   a. Who did the merchant have to bring to the Beast?
   b. What did the merchant promise to do if no one was willing to return with him?
   c. What would the Beast do if the merchant did not return?
3. The merchant left the next day.
   a. What did the merchant pick before he left?
   b. What did the Beast tell the merchant to take for Beauty?
   c. When was the merchant supposed to return to the Beast's palace?
   d. What animal took the merchant back to his cottage?
   e. Why did the merchant's children first think that his journey had gone well?
   f. What did the children want to do to the Beast?
   g. Why were the daughters angry with Beauty?
   h. Why did Beauty decide to go back with her father?
4. Write whether each statement describes the **merchant,** the **Beast, Beauty,** or one of **Beauty's sisters.**
   a. This character wanted jewels and dresses.
   b. This character asked for a rose.
   c. This character agreed to let somebody take his place.
   d. This character looked ugly.
   e. This character always tried to make the best of things.
   f. This character tried to pick a rose for somebody.
   g. This character lived all alone in a palace.
   h. This character agreed to take somebody's place.

PART E　Review Items

5. Use the words in the box to fill in the blanks or replace the underlined words.

in disguise	spacious	lining
inhabitants	abundant	crazy
dissatisfied	appetite	pity
astonishment	gleamed	greedy
vanished		

   a. Ruth was surprised and stared at the elephant with amazement.
   b. The whales are _____ of the ocean.
   c. The flies were so _____ that they covered the entire ceiling.
   d. Her clean hair shone and _____ in the sunlight.
   e. The rainy day made him very discontented.
   f. Bruce had lost his desire for food and the sight of food made him sick.
   g. Although people thought the beggar was very strange, nobody thought that he was insane.
   h. The child was so _____ that she took everything and then demanded more.
   i. When the wizard disappeared there was nothing left but his hat.
   j. The little boy cried, but nobody had any _____ for him.

PART F　Writing Assignment

Pretend you are Beauty. Would you have gone to stay with the Beast?

Write at least **four** sentences that explain your answer.

Lesson 82

PART A Word Lists

1
statue
chandelier
bracelet
portrait
grief
refuse

2
paw
pawing
patience
impatience

3
Vocabulary words
1. conceal
2. dread
3. hasty

4
Vocabulary words
1. long for
2. chandelier
3. portrait
4. grief
5. refuse

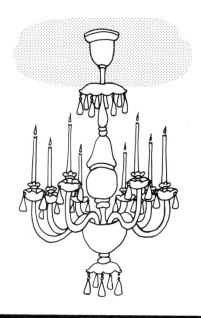

PART B Main Idea Paragraphs

Read the paragraph below. Then write a sentence that tells the main idea.

1.　　Dorothy walked into the clearing and gasped. A tin man was standing under a tree. He had an axe in his hands and a sad look on his face. Each one of his joints were rusted. His jaws were so rusted that he could only groan. Dorothy quickly figured out what the problem was and went to look for an oilcan. She found one in a shack and hurried back to the tin man. She oiled his jaws first. The tin man said, "How can I ever thank you?" Then Dorothy took care of the other joints.

PART C Story Items

2. **a.** What made the forest so light after night fell?
   b. Why was it strange that the forest was so warm?
   c. What did Beauty and her father find in the room with the fire?
3. **a.** What feeling did Beauty hide from the Beast?
   b. Why did the Beast ask Beauty if she had come willingly?

4. **a.** What did the Beast tell the merchant to take home to his children?
   b. Write the names of **two** things that Beauty and her father found in the cupboards.
   c. The more Beauty put in the trunks, the _____ room there seemed to be.
   d. Why did the merchant think that the Beast had deceived them?
   e. What kind of animal carried the trunks back to the merchant's cottage?
   f. Why was that animal unusual?
5. **a.** When did Beauty first see the Prince?
   b. What did he tell her not to trust much?
   c. Did Beauty understand her dream?
6. Write whether Beauty saw each thing in the **forest,** the **palace,** or her **dream.**
   a. A chest of gold
   b. Fireworks
   c. A brook bordered with trees
   d. A little room with a fireplace
   e. Wonderful colored lights
   f. A young prince
   g. Shelves full of jewels

PART D Review Items

7. Use the words in the box to fill in the blanks or replace the underlined words.

disappeared	sorrow	secure
got better	envy	abundant
amazement	desolate	frenzy
victims	persuade	linen
original		

a. His mouth fell open as he looked at the castle in astonishment.

b. Her mother made her Sunday dress out of _____.

c. Howard had wealth, but Sherry did not _____ him for having it.

d. The bridge was not safe and it fell apart.

e. She washed her hands and the stains vanished.

f. The story that the girl wrote was so clever that nobody believed that it was not a copy.

g. The patients in the hospital were _____ of a terrible accident.

h. There were no trees or plants on the barren desert.

i. The wounded man recovered quickly.

j. He could always _____ people to do what he wanted them to do.

PART E Writing Assignment

What do you think Beauty's dream means?

Write at least **four** sentences that explain your answer.

Lesson 83

PART A Word Lists

1
candlesticks
handsome
lifetime

2
Vocabulary words
1. long for
2. portrait
3. chandelier

PART B Main Idea Paragraphs

Read the paragraph below. Then write a sentence that tells the main idea.

1.   Just before noon, the Woodman went to the trees and began to work. He cut down the limbs of some trees, and then he chopped away all their twigs and leaves. He made a cart out of the limbs, and fastened it together with wooden pegs. Then he sliced four pieces from a big, round tree trunk and used the pieces for wheels. He worked so fast and well that by the time the mice began to arrive, the cart was all ready for them.

PART C Story Items

2. Beauty began to explore the palace.
   a. What did Beauty find hanging from a chandelier?
   b. Whose picture was on that object?
   c. Whose portrait did Beauty see in another room?
   d. Beauty sang in one room. What kind of objects were in that room?
   e. In what room did Beauty read?
3. a. On Beauty's first night in the palace, who came to see her?
   b. What did that character ask Beauty to do?
   c. What was Beauty's answer?

4. The next morning, Beauty went back to look at the portrait of the Prince.
   a. Why?
   b. Who did she think was a prisoner of the Beast?
5. Beauty saw the Beast again the next night.
   a. What question did the Beast ask Beauty again?
   b. What was Beauty's answer?
   c. How did that answer seem to make the Beast feel?
6. a. Where did Beauty ask the Beast to send her?
   b. How long would Beauty be gone?
   c. What did the Beast say would happen if Beauty did not come back in time?
   d. What object did the Beast tell Beauty would bring her back to the palace?
   e. What did Beauty have to say to that object when she was ready to return?
7. Beauty had another dream that night.
   a. What did the Prince say might happen if Beauty left?
   b. Who did Beauty say that she would die for?

PART D   Review Items

8. Write which god each statement describes. Choose from **Jupiter, Mercury** or **Neptune.**
   a. He was the chief Roman god.
   b. He was the Roman messenger god.
   c. He was the Roman god of the sea.

9. Use the words in the box to fill in the blanks or replace the underlined words.

concealed	greedy
inhabitant	poverty
greatly frightened	frenzy
spacious	hated
pitied	insane
selfish	envy

   a. You are an ——————— of the planet Earth.
   b. The beehive fell to the ground and the bees came out in a <u>hurried and excited way</u>.
   c. People <u>felt sorrow for</u> the friendly man because he was so poor and lonely.
   d. The dog scratched the door during its <u>crazy</u> rage.
   e. After King Midas lost something he loved very much, he was not so ——————— for gold.
   f. The woman was <u>terrified</u> by the fierce lion.
   g. Two of the children were quite thoughtful, but one was <u>concerned only with herself</u>.
   h. Ruth did not complain about being poor and hungry because she had never known anything but

      ———————.
   i. Tina's vacation had been exciting and she <u>dreaded</u> going back to school.
   j. The pirates had <u>hidden</u> their treasure somewhere on the island.

PART E   Writing Assignment

Do you think that Beauty should marry the Beast?

Write at least **four** sentences that explain your answer.

Lesson 84

PART A Word Lists

1
produce
semi
reassured
warehouse
lettuce
wad

2
joyfully
constantly
loudly
dearly
apparently

3
Vocabulary words
1. trust appearances
2. trace of
3. spell
4. despite
5. warehouse

PART B Main Idea Paragraphs

Read the paragraph below. Then write a sentence that tells the main idea.

1.   The Guardian of the Gates opened the big, green box, and Dorothy saw that it was filled with spectacles of every size and shape. All of them were made out of green glass. The green man found a pair that fit Dorothy and put them over her eyes. The spectacles had two golden bands fastened to them that passed around the back of Dorothy's head. The Guardian of the Gates locked the bands together with a little key that was at the end of a chain that he wore around his neck.

PART C Story Items

2. a. Whose house was Beauty in when she woke up?
   b. How do you think Beauty got there?
   c. How did Beauty's family first feel when they first saw her again?
   d. Who told Beauty what her dream meant?
   e. What did that person think that Beauty should do?
   f. Who did Beauty want to marry?
3. a. How long did Beauty stay at her father's house?
   b. Which members of her family were used to being without Beauty?

c. On the night that Beauty was to return to the palace, she had

_____.
   ● a happy dream   ● no dream
   ● a dismal dream

4. a. Where did she find the Beast in her dream?
   b. What was happening to him?
   c. What did Beauty decide to do the next morning?
   d. What did Beauty do to her ring that night?
5. a. When Beauty was back in the palace, why was she upset before supper?
   b. Why did she run into the garden?
   c. Where did she find the Beast?
   d. Where had Beauty seen that place before?
6. The Beast was lying on the ground.
   a. What did Beauty sprinkle over him?
   b. Beauty said, "I never knew how much I _____ you until now."
7. The Beast later visited Beauty.
   a. What did the Beast ask her to do?
   b. What was Beauty's answer?
   c. What happened to the Beast when Beauty gave that answer?
8. a. Who had put a spell on the Prince?
   b. What had the spell changed the Prince into?
   c. What kind of person could change the Prince back?
   d. How did that person have to feel about the Prince?
   e. Why was it difficult for any person to feel that way about the Beast?
   f. Who had broken the witch's spell?
   g. What happened the next day?

PART D   Review Items

9. Use the words in the box to fill in the blanks or replace the underlined words.

great sorrow	hasty
persuade	victim
vanished	recover
selfish	schedule
occupied	deceived
deserted	original
mechanic	

a. The players were deeply <u>busy</u> with their game of checkers.
b. Tom's dog had <u>disappeared</u> and could not be found.
c. Experts first thought that the painting was a copy, but later they discovered it was an _____.
d. The man tried to _____ shoppers to buy things at his store.
e. The silent plains were lonely and <u>desolate</u>.
f. She lay down to <u>get better</u> from the hard work.
g. The boy would not share his toys because he was so _____.
h. The frightened horse fled in a <u>quick</u> gallop.
i. Matt was <u>tricked</u> into giving all his money to thieves.
j. The woman felt <u>grief</u> when she was fired from her job.

PART E   Writing Assignment

Do you know anybody like Beauty and the Beast?

Write at least **four** sentences that explain your answer.

Lesson 85

PART A   Word Lists

1	2	3	4	5
Carlos Hernandez	railroad	semi	wring	**Vocabulary words**
tomato	handcart	semis	dinner	1. trace of
crayon	ourselves	trail	diner	2. trust appearances
	cardboard	trailer	wringing	3. despite
		Bugsy	assured	4. warehouse
		wad	reassured	5. spell
		wade		

PART B   Main Idea Paragraphs

Read the paragraph below. Then write a sentence that tells the main idea.

1.   When the Beast did not appear, Beauty was frightened. After listening and waiting for a long time, she ran down into the garden to search for the Beast. Up and down the paths poor Beauty ran, calling for the Beast. No one answered, and she could not find a trace of him. At last, she stopped for a minute's rest, and saw that she was standing near the cave she had seen in her dreams. She entered the cave, and sure enough, there was the Beast, fast asleep. Beauty was glad to have found him.

PART C   Story Items

2. **a.** Write the name of the company the narrator worked for.
   b. During what season did the narrator work for that company?
   c. What did the narrator do the rest of the year?

3. **a.** What are the large trucks that come to the produce docks called?
   b. The truck drivers wanted the crew to work quickly, so they could
   _____ .
   - take a rest
   - fix their trucks
   - get on the road

4. **a.** Who always yelled at the crew to work faster?
   b. Who was the leader of the crew?
   - Mr. Olson   • The narrator
   - Arnold Bing

5. Write the names of **four** types of produce.

6. **a.** What was the name of the new man who came to work on the crew?
   b. What was different about the way that person worked?
   c. When Carlos was working at first, the narrator felt embarrassed. Why?

7. Pretty soon all the members of the crew except one began to work fast.
   a. Who didn't work fast?
   b. How long did it take Carlos and the crew to unload the first truck?

8. **a.** After Carlos and the crew unloaded a truck in one hour and ten minutes, what did the crew at the next dock say they could do?
   b. Did they do that?
   c. So what did Carlos's crew do?
   d. Another crew set a record at forty-eight minutes. Where was that crew?
   e. Finally, Carlos's crew set a record that nobody beat. What was that record?
   - 30 minutes   • 43 minutes
   - one hour and 10 minutes

9. What did Carlos write the crew's record on?

10. **a.** When the crew worked faster, Mr. Olson got _____ business.
    - less   • the same   • more
    b. Mister Olson began to treat the crew as if they were his _____ .

PART D   Review Items

11. **Use the words in the box to fill in the blanks or replace the underlined words.**

secure	refused	hid
disappeared	poverty	grief
terrified	persuade	victim
unhappy	complain	

   a. When the cat chased the chipmunk, it <u>vanished</u> into a hole.
   b. The panting dog was a _____ of the heat.
   c. Once Ellen had made up her mind, they could not _____ her to change it.
   d. The evil ghost <u>greatly frightened</u> many people.
   e. That humble beggar is a victim of _____ .
   f. Hilda <u>concealed</u> her father's birthday present in the closet.
   g. Danny thought of his lonely childhood with <u>great sorrow</u>.
   h. The old horse _____ to pull such a heavy wagon, so she just stood still.

PART E   Writing Assignment

What kind of job would you like to have?

Write at least **four** sentences that explain your answer.

Lesson 86

PART A   Word Lists

1
suburbs
mayor
Italian
Russian
exist
memory

2
Halsted Street
Maria Rossi
Hull House
Chicago
Michigan

3
Vocabulary words
1. suburbs
2. slum
3. mayor

PART B   Main Idea Paragraphs

Read the paragraph below. Then write a sentence that tells the main idea.

1.   Oz is a Great Wizard, and can take on any form he wishes. Some say he looks like a bird, and some say he looks like an elephant, and some say he looks like a cat. To others he appears as a beautiful princess, or in any other form that pleases him. But no one knows who the real Oz is or when he is in his own form.

PART C   Story Items

2. a. Who is the main character in this biography?
   b. Which city did that character live in?
   c. What street is exactly one mile west of downtown?
   d. What is the name of the museum on that street?
3. Different narrators tell the story of Jane Addams.
   a. Are the narrators real people or fictional people?
   b. Are the events they tell about real events or fictional events?
4. a. Who is the first narrator?
   b. How many children were in Maria's family?
   c. How many rooms did Maria's house have?
   d. How old were the children when they started to work?
   e. Where did Maria work?

5. a. Were the people in Maria's neighborhood rich or poor?
   b. Which language did Maria's parents speak?
   c. Which country had the people on Maria's street come from?
6. a. At what time did Maria go to work in the morning?
   b. What time did she finish work in the evening?
   c. How many hours did she work each day?
7. a. Why did the street have a bad smell in the summertime?
   b. Write the names of **two** kinds of animals that swarmed around the garbage.
   c. Why did Maria's family have traps in their house?

PART D   Review Items

8. Complete the moral for each story.
   a. The Miraculous Pitcher:
      Be _____ to strangers.
   b. The Golden Touch:
      _____ is better than
      _____.
   c. Beauty and the Beast:
      Do not trust _____.

9. Use the words in the box to fill in the blanks or replace the underlined words.

get better	quick	hated
abundant	trace of	hid
breathe in	refuse	trick

a. She was so tired that she <u>dreaded</u> the thought of doing more work.

b. There was no time for anything, but a <u>hasty</u> shower.

c. No one could <u>deceive</u> her because she was very wise.

d. Lynn did not want to go to the party, but she could not _____ their invitation.

e. At last the hound dog lost the scent and could no longer find a _____ it.

PART E   Writing Assignment

Maria said that her neighborhood was not all bad.

Write at least **three** things that you think she might like about it.

Lesson 87

PART A   Word Lists

1
Buon Giorno
sausage
agile
nowhere
sewing
Gino

2
pitifully
instantly
bitterly
politely

3
Vocabulary words
1. slum
2. mayor
3. suburbs

4
Vocabulary words
1. peddler
2. rumor
3. foreman
4. agile
5. flattering

PART B   Main Idea Paragraphs

Read the paragraph below. Then write a sentence that tells the main idea.

1.   The woman told the man that she did not like his wild ways. When they got married she picked out a nice dry cave to live in, and she lit a nice fire at the back of the cave. Then she spread clean sand on the floor and said, "Wipe your feet, dear, when you come in, and now we'll keep house."

PART C   Story Items

2. a. The merchants who came down Maria's street were called

_____.

b. Write the names of at least **three** things those merchants sold.

c. Which merchant would Maria like to follow in the summertime?

d. What would Maria get when she followed that merchant?

3. a. On Sundays, Maria's family would go on _____.

b. Which lake would they go to?

c. On their way to the lake, they would go through _____.
- a farm
- downtown
- a suburb
- Chicago

d. Name one way that part of the city was different from Maria's neighborhood.

e. Maria said that the picnic was not really over when she went home. Why wasn't it really over for Maria?

4. Maria described what it was like to wake up in the morning.
   a. Name at least **two** noises that she would hear.
   b. Which language did the people in Maria's neighborhood speak?

5. a. What would Maria's mother argue about with peddlers?
   b. Why would the people stop to watch the argument?
   c. Did anybody pay the prices that the peddler first asked?

6. Maria walked to work.
   a. Which street did she walk on?
   b. Which house did she pass?
   c. What kind of factory did she work in?
   d. Which language did she have to speak in that factory?

PART D   Review Items

7. a. What is the name of the city you are reading about?
   b. Which street is exactly one mile west of downtown?
   c. What was the name of the large house on that street?
   d. The neighborhoods that surrounded the house were _____ .
      ● rich   ● poor

e. Write the names of **two** countries that the people in those neighborhoods came from.

8. a. Who is the narrator of the first part of the biography?
   b. Who is the main character of the biography?

9. **Use the words in the box to fill in the blanks or replace the underlined words.**

tricked	linen
greatly frightened	gleam
trace of	persuade
dreaded	despite

a. The puppy would beg and _____ people to pet him.
b. The owl hated bright lights.
c. The fox deceived the hounds and escaped.
d. Her footprints in the sand were the only _____ her.
e. The ball game was played _____ the rain.

PART E   Writing Assignment

Every neighborhood has different noises.

Write at least **five** sentences that describe the sounds in your neighborhood early in the morning.

Lesson 88

PART A   Word Lists

1	2
kindergarten	**Vocabulary words**
sewing	1. flattering
Gino	2. agile
crayon	3. peddler
wad	4. foreman
nowhere	5. rumor

PART B   Story Items

1. **a.** The factory that Maria worked in made _____.
   b. What happened if you were one minute late for work?
   c. How did Maria like the smell of the candy when she first started working in the factory?
   d. How did Maria like the smell of the candy after a while?
   e. Who yelled at Maria if she stopped working for a moment?
   f. How many hours a day did Maria work?

2. Two rich women moved into the neighborhood.
   a. Write the names of those two women.
   b. In what year did they move in?
   c. They wanted to turn the old house into a _____.
   - warehouse   • suburb
   - settlement house
   d. What were the women going to start for young children?
   e. What language were the women going to teach?
   f. Name two other kinds of classes the women were going to offer.

3. **a.** What person didn't believe that the women had really opened a kindergarten?
   b. How many kindergartens were there in the neighborhood before Hull House opened.

4. One day, Maria went into Hull House.
   a. Name two foreign languages Maria heard inside the house.
   b. What was the furniture like?
   c. Who did Maria talk to?
   d. Maria asked if somebody could go to the kindergarten. Who was that person?
   e. What was Maria's family invited to do?

5. Write whether each statement describes **Maria's neighborhood,** the **factory,** or **Hull House.**
   a. There were boxes filled with garbage.
   b. It had expensive furniture.
   c. Young children could go to school there.
   d. The smell was very sweet.
   e. Rats and insects were everywhere.
   f. A foreman would yell when somebody stopped working.
   g. People learned how to speak English there.
   h. People had to speak English there.

PART C   Review Items

6. **Use the words in the box to fill in the blanks or replace the underlined words.**

great sorrow	suburb	safe
originals	mayor	crazy
despite	conceal	slum

   a. She lived in a very nice _____ of the city.
   b. She put on a disguise to <u>hide</u> herself.
   c. When he realized that he would have to leave his friends, he was overcome with <u>grief</u>.
   d. Jacob decided to join the others _____ his bad feelings about them.
   e. Some of the houses in the crowded _____ were quite dilapidated.
   f. Mr. Brown was elected _____ of the city.

PART D   Writing Assignment

Would you like to work in a factory?

Write at least **five** sentences that explain your answer.

Lesson 89

PART A   Word Lists

1	2	3
soot	agile	**Vocabulary words**
community	fashion	1. chimney
Europe	fashioned	2. soot
		3. shawl
		4. draped

PART B   Story Items

1. In what year did Hull House open?
2. a. How did Maria's family heat their house?
   b. Why did they put blankets over their windows?
   c. At night, the inside of their house got nearly as cold as the _____.
3. Maria's mother started going to Hull House.
   a. Which class did she help out in?
   b. Which class did she always say she was going to take, but never did?
4. One evening, Maria met a group of her friends.
   a. What kind of clothes were her friends dressed in?
   b. Where were they going?
   c. What were they going to do there?
5. a. Who had first owned the dress Maria wore on Sunday?
   b. Why didn't Maria want anybody to look at her feet?
   c. How did the people in the audience like the singing?
   d. What did Jane Addams offer the girls after they sang?
   e. Why did the girls refuse it?
   f. Where did Jane Addams think the girls should spend their days?
6. a. Who helped change the situation in the factories?
   b. How old did children have to be to work in factories after 1893?
   c. Why didn't the new law help Maria?

7. Write whether each statement describes Maria's neighborhood **before** Hull House opened or **after** Hull House opened. Write **before** or **after** for each statement.
   a. Twelve-year-old children worked in factories.
   b. Very few people spoke English.
   c. Children started going to school.
   d. People started to feel like neighbors.
   e. People learned new skills.

PART C   Review Items

8. Write the name of the character each statement describes. Choose from the **Cat that Walked,** the **Ugly Duckling, Buck, Nellie, Brown Wolf,** or **Martha.**
   a. This character pulled a thousand-pound sled.
   b. This character found somebody with its nose.
   c. This character jumped over fences.
   d. This character decided to go back to the Klondike.
   e. This character discovered that it could fly.
   f. This character made a bargain with a woman.

9. Use the words in the box to fill in the blanks or replace the underlined words.

desire for food	dread
figure out	refused
suburb	agile
rumors	fury

a. Those soldiers will go into battle but they will <u>hate</u> the fighting.

b. The man was so tired that he _____ to walk another step.

c. He moved from the center of New York City to the _____ .

d. They said that she was the most nimble and _____ dancer they had ever seen.

e. Some of the things he said were true, but most of them were nothing but _____ .

PART D Writing Assignment

What kind of classes would you like to have taken at Hull House?

Write at least **five** sentences that explain your answer.

Lesson 90

PART A Word Lists

1	2	3	4
resident	exhibit	**Vocabulary words**	**Vocabulary words**
fascinated	nurse	1. shawl	1. resident
supervisor	nursery	2. draped	2. fascinated
infant	soup	3. soot	3. ward
dedicated	soot		4. profit
Irish	community		5. supervisor
			6. infant

PART B Main Idea Paragraphs

Read the paragraph below. Then write a sentence that tells the main idea.

1. Beauty and her father went into the next room, which had shelves and cupboards all around it. They were greatly surprised at the riches the room contained. They went from cupboard to cupboard, selecting precious things, which they heaped into two trunks. The trunks were soon so heavy that an elephant could not have carried them.

PART C Story Items

2. a. Who heard Jane Addams give a talk at a club meeting downtown?

b. In what year was that?
 • 1910 • 1893 • 1860

c. Jane Addams talked about a law. What was the law going to prevent children under fourteen years old from doing?

d. Jane Addams told a story about a boy. What happened to that boy?

e. Where did Jane Addams think that boy should have been?

f. For how many years had Jane Addams and her friends been trying to change the law?

3. a. Which ward was Hull House in?

b. Who made that ward famous?

c. Jane Addams said, "Hull House is a _____ bringing neighbors together."
- bridge
- prison
- factory

4. a. Who was interested in becoming a resident at Hull House?

b. Did most of the residents have regular jobs?

c. Did the residents earn money working at Hull House?

5. Rita thought that the poor people in Ward 19 had some of the same problems another group of people had.

a. Which group was that?
- women
- bankers
- men

b. Name **two** things that Rita couldn't do because she was a woman.

c. Rita thought that if she worked for Hull House, she would be doing things that are _____ .
- unimportant
- important
- boring

d. Who made the mistake that Rita was blamed for?

6. Rita described her cab ride.

a. Where was she going?

b. About how far did she have to go?

c. Which street was lined with little shops?

d. Why did the cab go slowly on that street?

PART D   Review Items

7. You have been reading about Jane Addams.

a. Which city did she live in?

b. Which street is one mile west of downtown?

c. What was the name of the house that she opened on that street?

d. Were the neighborhoods near that house rich or poor?

e. Name **two** countries that people in that neighborhood came from.

8. Use the words in the box to fill in the blanks or replace the underlined words.

mayor	fury	grief	envy
soot	refused	agile	slum

a. News of the dead cat brought <u>great sorrow</u> to the children.

b. She did not want to work in a factory, so she _____ the job offer.

c. By saving all her money, she managed to move from a _____ to a village near the city.

d. The _____ makes decisions about how to run the city.

e. Only a very _____ dog can jump through a high hoop.

PART E   Writing Assignment

Rita felt that women were not treated fairly in 1893. Do you think that's still true?

Write at least **five** sentences that explain your answer.

Lesson 91

PART A Word Lists

1	2	3	4
donate	range	**Vocabulary words**	**Vocabulary words**
stubborn	arrange	1. ward	1. donate
inspector	sicken	2. supervisor	2. filth
fiery	sickening	3. infant	3. stubborn
wages		4. resident	4. fined
		5. fascinated	
		6. profit	

PART B Main Idea Paragraphs

Read the paragraph below. Then write a sentence that tells the main idea.

1. The Parkers walked up to the ticket window. Mrs. Parker said, "Two adults and two children, please." Mrs Parker gave the tickets to the usher, then Mr. Parker took the kids over to the popcorn stand. A few minutes later, the Parkers settled into some seats in the middle of the theater. The house lights went out, and some pictures flashed on to the screen. The Parkers saw an evil monster being zapped by a woman in a space suit. They saw lots of spaceships and computers. After about two hours, the words, "The End" came on the screen, and the house lights went back on. The Parkers got up to leave.

PART C Story Items

2. a. In what year did Rita Hansen get a job at Hull House?
    b. At Hull House, Rita worked as a

    _____ .

    c. Where did Rita work during the day?
    d. Did she feel that her day job was important?
3. a. What was one of the biggest problems in the neighborhood?
      ● garbage collection   ● crime
      ● potholes
    b. Why did Rita need to make speeches?
4. One of Rita's speeches stirred up trouble.
    a. Which person did Rita criticize in that speech?
    b. What did that person own in Ward 19?
    c. What condition was that property in?
5. a. Were Rita's parents rich or poor?
    b. At first, how did Rita's parents feel about her job at Hull House?
    c. What did Rita's parents invite Rita to give at their house?
6. a. Which law was the city of Chicago going to pass?
      ● a driving law   ● a housing law
      ● a factory law
    b. Who was going to be a factory inspector?

7. Write whether Rita would consider each of the following jobs **important** or **unimportant.**
   a. Counting money at the bank
   b. Changing twenty dollar bills
   c. Talking to poor people about their problems
   d. Adding up numbers on an adding machine
   e. Making speeches to raise money for Hull House
   f. Teaching English to foreigners

8. Write **fact** or **fiction** for each statement.
   a. The Greeks believed that Zeus was the chief god.
   b. Zeus talked to people.
   c. Jane Addams started Hull House.
   d. The Beast changed into a Prince.

PART E   Writing Assignment

Pretend you are making a speech to raise money for Hull House.

Write at least **six** sentences of that speech.

Lesson 92

PART A   Word Lists

1	2	3	4
investor	dilapidated	**Vocabulary words**	**Vocabulary words**
collector	wages	1. stubborn	1. abandon
inspector	sober	2. donate	2. invest
manager	vigorous	2. filth	3. wages
supervisor	abandon	4. fined	4. distressed
	spectacular		5. trance
			6. vigorous
			7. plump

PART B Main Idea Paragraphs

Read the paragraph below. Then write a sentence that tells the main idea.

1.   Juan got a book out of the library last Monday. The book was a novel, and the main character was a spider. After school on Tuesday, Juan opened the book and saw that it had four parts. He decided to read one part each day. He finished the first part later that night, and he could hardly wait to read part two on Wednesday. But he had to go out on Wednesday night, so he didn't get to read part two until Thursday. Juan finally finished part four on Saturday afternoon. He closed the book and took it back to the library.

PART C   Story Items

2. **a.** Where did Rita Hansen give a speech?
   b. Write the name of the person who got angry after the speech
   c. What business did that person own?
   d. Name a person who worked at that factory.
3. **a.** The owner said that somebody was threatening his business. Who was that person?
   b. Why did Rita's father step between Rita and the man?
   c. Whose side was Rita's father on?
4. **a.** In what year did Camila Perez go to Chicago?
   b. How old was Jane Addams that year?
   c. How many years had passed since Jane Addams opened Hull House?
   - 46 years   • 60 years
   - 10 years
   d. What was different about the street lights in 1935?
   e. How many buildings did Hull House have in 1935?
5. Camila Perez told about problems in the United States.
   a. There was a terrible _____ in 1935.
   b. Was the situation getting worse or better in 1935?
6. How did Camila Perez get from New York to Chicago?
7. **a.** Who did Camila think about on her trip?
   b. What were the people who lived in Hull House called?
8. **a.** What did Jane Addams try to stop in 1914?
   b. In what year did World War One end?
   c. What did Jane Addams do just after the war ended?
   d. Jane Addams said, "All the people in the world are _____."

PART D   Review Items

9. **Use the words in the box to fill in the blanks or replace the underlined words.**

fascinated	rumor
terrify	agile
unhappy	deceived
infant	abundant
profit	boss
resident	

   a. Everyone had heard the mysterious _____ that Nancy told.
   b. She was sad, but her friends were <u>tricked</u> by her smile.
   c. A tightrope walker should be very <u>nimble</u>.
   d. She was not a _____ of the state of Texas.
   e. The cat was <u>interested and delighted</u> by the mice.
   f. With the _____ from her business, she bought a new car.
   g. Her <u>supervisor</u> made sure that she was <u>doing her work</u>.
   h. The hungry <u>baby</u> wailed for its mother.

PART E   Writing Assignment

When Camila meets Jane Addams, she will ask Jane some questions. Write at least two questions that you think Camila will ask. Then write Jane's answers.

Lesson 93

PART A   Word Lists

1	**2**	**3** Vocabulary words	**4** Vocabulary words
surround	stubborn	1. trance	1. interview
picture	month	2. wages	2. spectacular
courage	plumbing	3. distressed	
scurry		4. plump	
harbor		5. invest	
		6. vigorous	
		7. abandon	

PART B   Main Idea Paragraphs

Read the paragraph below. Then write a sentence that tells the main idea.

1.   Sylvia looked out her window and said, "What a perfect day for drawing." So she selected a big piece of paper and several different pencils. Then she went outside and started drawing. She made an outline, then she drew in the details. She showed a man walking down the street and some kids playing near the fire hydrant. She drew for almost four hours. Finally, she said, "It's finished."

PART C   Story Items

2. Camila Perez told about some of the things Jane Addams had done.
   a. Which war left many people starving in Europe?
   b. Jane Addams said, "We must be good _____."
      • neighbors   • fighters
      • athletes
   c. Which award did Jane Addams receive in 1931?
   d. Did Jane Addams stop working as hard when her health failed?
3. a. Who did Camila Perez finally meet in the afternoon?
   b. Who did that person visit after Camila's interview?
   c. What happened to Jane Addams a week after Camila talked with her?
   d. In what year did Jane Addams die?
4. Camila Perez said that Jane Addams was not really dead because she lived in people's _____.

PART D   Review Items

5. **Use the words in the box to fill in the blanks or replace the underlined words.**

victim	rumor
stubborn	filth
profit	gave
interested and delighted	

   a. The sound of her voice fascinated him so much that he could not stop listening to her.
   b. Jennifer no longer needed those things, so she donated them to the settlement house.
   c. Odessa heard a _____ that the president was bald.
   d. They gave their dog a bath because he was covered with dirt.
   e. She was so _____ that she would not smile, no matter how nice they were to her.

PART E   Writing Assignment

What do you think cities should do with buildings that are in bad condition?

Write at least **five** sentences that explain your answer.

Lesson 94

PART A   Word Lists

1
opportunity
pauper

2
Vocabulary words
1. spectacular
2. interview

3
Vocabulary words
1. hardware
2. harbor
3. pauper
4. plumbing
5. prince
6. scurry

PART B   Main Idea Paragraphs

Read the paragraph below. Then write a sentence that tells the main idea.

1.   Mrs. Putnam flicked on her old radio. Nothing happened. She checked the plug, but it was fine. So she unplugged the radio and took the back off with a screwdriver. She noticed that a wire was loose. Mrs. Putnam tightened the wire and put the back on again. Then she plugged the radio in. It worked. Mrs. Putnam smiled to herself and said, "I just saved a trip to the service center."

PART C   Story Items

2. **a.** What's the title of the next novel you will read?
   b. In which country does the novel take place?
   c. During which years does the novel take place?
3. **a.** Why did people have to buy water from peddlers?
   b. What kinds of traps did some peddlers sell?

4. **a.** Explain why wagons often got stuck on the roads.
   b. Why did travelers carry swords or guns on the roads?
   c. Which travelers went the fastest on the roads?
5. **a.** Why were so many poor farmers forced off their land?
   b. What famous saying did the poor farmers have?
6. **a.** Name three uses people had for wood.
   b. Was the demand for wood high or low?
   c. So what happened to some forests?
7. **a.** What did people use coal for?
   b. What metal did people make in blast furnaces?

PART D   Review Items

8. Use the words in the box to fill in the blanks or replace the underlined words.

accused of	profit
residents	hate
distressed	plump
agile	donate
infant	hide
abandoned	

a. Paul was not only strong; he was also very quick and <u>nimble</u>.

b. Her parents had died when she was just an _____.

c. Seven _____ of that hotel went up to the roof for a party.

d. The businessman made a large _____ from his investment.

e. Because she hurt her ankle, the runner _____ the race.

f. They pleaded with the man, but he would not <u>give</u> any money to the organization.

g. Their fighting <u>troubled</u> her, and she begged them <u>to stop</u>.

h. The well-fed puppies were round and a <u>little fat</u>.

PART E   Writing Assignment

Write a paragraph that compares life in the 1500's with your life today. Tell how they are different and how they are the same.

Make your paragraph at least **five** sentences long.

Lesson 95

PART A   Word Lists

1
opportunity
optimistic
earl
Tudor

2
Vocabulary words
1. scurry
2. hardware
3. plumbing
4. pauper
5. prince

3
Vocabulary words
1. ruler
2. opportunity

PART B Main Idea Paragraphs

Read the paragraph below. Then write a
sentence that tells the main idea.

1.   Darlene looked at the mountain
looming up before her. She had never
seen Mount Whitney before, and she
could hardly wait to get to the top of it.
She parked her car and started up the
trail. The spring weather was beautiful.
Flowers were blossoming, and little
animals could be seen everywhere.
Darlene went higher and higher. The
trail became more and more difficult.
Toward the top, the trail broke down
altogether and Darlene had to climb
over several big rocks. Finally, Darlene
reached the peak. The view nearly took
her breath away.

PART C Story Items

2. a. In 1501, England was ruled by
Henry the _____.
   • Sixth   • Seventh   • Eighth
   b. Who was the richest man in England
in 1501?
   c. How was the Prince of Wales related
to the king?
   d. Which person was the Prince of
Wales in 1501?
3. The lords and ladies used different
titles.
   a. The wife of a duke was called
a _____.
   b. The husband of a countess was
called a _____.
   c. Name two other titles of lords or
ladies.
4. a. Which king ruled England from
1509 to 1547?
   b. What happened to people who
criticized this king?
   c. How many wives did this king
have?
   d. What saying did people use to
remember all the wives?

5. The names of the king's three children
were Elizabeth, Edward, and Mary.
   a. Which child became the ruler of
England right after the king died?
   b. Which child became the last Tudor
ruler?
   c. What nickname did one of the
children get?
   d. Why did the child get that
nickname?
6. a. Which Tudor encouraged English
sailors to explore the world?
   b. Why were writers happier during
Elizabeth's rule?
   c. Who was the most famous writer?
   d. Why was Elizabeth the last Tudor?

PART D   Review Items

7. Use the words in the box to fill in the blanks or replace the underlined words.

garbage and dirt	invested
wages	vigorous
insane	fascinated
despite	supervisor
appetite	rumor

a. The man heard a _____ that someone had found his lost dog.

b. Some programs on television <u>interested and delighted the little girl and she watched them</u> regularly.

c. Bob received his paycheck from his <u>boss.</u>

d. In 1893, many slums were full of <u>filth.</u>

e. The rich woman had _____ all of her money in business deals.

f. Gail never had enough money because her _____ were only fifty dollars a week.

g. Running is <u>lively</u> exercise.

PART E   Writing Assignment

How would you feel if our country was ruled by a king or a queen? Write a paragraph that explains your answer.

Make your paragraph at least **five** sentences long.

Lesson 96

PART A   Word Lists

1
collector
manager
investor
supervisor
inspector

2
Vocabulary words
1. opportunity
2. ruler

3
Vocabulary words
1. carve
2. properly

PART B   Story Items

1. a. What were the two main classes of people in England in the 1500's?
   b. Which class were the lords and ladies in?
   c. Which class were the farmers in?

2. About how many people lived in a lord's house?
   ● 5   ● 15   ● 50   ● 500

3. a. How were the rooms heated?
   b. Why wasn't there much furniture?
   c. Name two ways the beds were different from modern beds.

4. a. Who was the master of the house?
   b. Which person had the job of running the house?
   c. Name at least two products that were made in the house.

d. Why were those products made in the house?

5. a. What was the main thing that rich people ate?
   b. What new vegetable did they begin to eat in the 1580's?

6. a. Which of the following words describe clothes worn by the rich people?
   fancy   inexpensive   practical   jeweled   costly
   b. Name some of the sports and hobbies that rich people had.
   c. Why were many rich people able to buy books for the first time?

7. a. Where did rich people sit when they watched plays in theaters?
   b. Which famous playwright began writing plays in the 1500's?

PART C   Review Items

8. Use the words in the box to fill in the blanks or replace the underlined words.

stubborn	scampered	give
get better	distressed	persuade
spectacular	investing	infants

a. Felicia looked at him with sad and <u>troubled</u> eyes.

b. The shortstop made a <u>very impressive</u> catch.

c. They told him to stop trying, but he was so _____ that he would not quit.

d. She heard that she could make a large profit by _____ money in the property.

e. Irving was late so he <u>scurried</u> to school.

f. Most adults cannot remember being _____.

PART D   Writing Assignment

Pretend you are a kitchen servant in a lord's house. Write a paragraph that describes what your life is like. Tell what you do all day long. Also tell how you feel about your master.

Make your paragraph at least **five** sentences long.

PART E   Special Projects

1. Jane Addams solved many problems in Ward 19. She put children in school; she built a playground; she made sure the garbage was picked up; she made sure factories didn't hire children.

   Think about some of the problems that you have in your town. Get together with other students and make up a list of at least three problems. Write the list of problems on a large piece of paper. Then try to come up with a solution for each problem. When you agree on a solution, write it next to the problem. Finally, write a few sentences that explain why each solution will work. When you finish, you will have a large poster that shows several problems and solutions. Show the poster to the rest of the class and find out if they agree with your solutions.

2. "The Miraculous Pitcher," "The Golden Touch," and "Beauty and the Beast" all had morals. Write a story that has a moral. Make your story at least twenty sentences long. When you finish the story, read it to the rest of the class and ask them what they think the moral is.

   Here are some morals you might want to use:
   - It is better to give than to receive.
   - A penny saved is a penny earned.
   - Don't put all your hopes on just one thing.
   - Don't complain about what has already happened.

   You can also think up your own moral.

Lesson 97

PART A   Word Lists

1
Vocabulary
1. spectacular
2. opportunity
3. properly

2
New vocabulary
1. confine
2. humble
3. optimistic

PART B   Main Idea Paragraphs

Read the paragraph below. Then write a sentence that tells the main idea.

1.   Andre was tired of the drab green walls in his room. He got some money from his father, then he went to the hardware store and bought a can of bright blue paint and a paintbrush. When he got home, he set to work right away. He decided to start with the west wall. He dipped the brush into the paint and began to spread the paint across the wall. Bit by bit, the wall turned from drab green to bright blue. Andrew worked for a long time. By the end of the day, the room was finished and the paint was all gone.

PART C   Story Items

2. a. Why did so many poor farmers lose their land?
   b. What did most poor farmers do after they lost their land?
   c. Which ruler finally helped the poor farmers?

3. a. How many rooms did a farmhouse have?
   b. What was the roof of a farmhouse made out of?
   c. Why didn't the farmers eat at a table?
   d. Where did the farmers sleep?
4. a. What materials were poor people's clothes made of?
   b. Why didn't poor people wear fancy shoes or socks?
5. a. What happened to robbers who killed rich people?
   b. What other punishments did robbers receive?
   c. What device were homeless people put into?
   d. What device were certain women put into?
6. Why did poor people like Elizabeth better than they liked Henry the Eighth?
7. a. Is *The Prince and the Pauper* fact or fiction?
   b. Name two characters in the book who are not fictional.

PART D   Review Items

8. Use the words in the box to fill in the blanks or replace the underlined words.

opportunity	pauper
mayor	vigorous
wages	abandoned
troubled	figure out
infant	

a. As the rain continued, the people in the castle became more and more <u>distressed</u>.

b. By the time he paid all the money he owed, he had nothing left from his _____.

c. The man took the <u>chance</u> to invest his money.

d. Because he had lost all his money, the man was a _____.

e. When their plan would not work, they _____ it.

f. Nellie ran and jumped over the fence with one <u>lively</u> leap.

PART E   Writing Assignment

If you were a judge today, what kind of punishment would you give a robber? Write a paragraph that explains your answer. Describe how the punishment would work. Also tell how it would stop the robber from robbing.

Make your paragraph at least **five** sentences long.

Lesson 98

PART A   Word Lists

1	**2**	**3**	**4**
presence	jewel	**Vocabulary review**	**New vocabulary**
gifted	ancient	1. confine	1. ignorant
abilities	beggar	2. humble	2. unleash
wisdom	jeweled		3. ability
Westminster	ate		4. gifted
	create		5. wisdom
	imitation		
	dilapidated		

PART B   New Vocabulary

1. ignorant—If a person is **ignorant,** that person does not understand things. A person who does not understand arithmetic is **ignorant** about arithmetic.

- A person who does not understand steeplechases is _____.

2. unleash—When you **unleash** something, you let it run free. If you let your feelings run free, you **unleash** your feelings.

- If you let your imagination run free, you _____.

3. **ability**—If you have the **ability** to do something, you are able to do that thing. If you are able to write, you have the **ability** to write.
   - If you can run as fast as a dog, you _____.

4. **gifted**—Somebody who has a lot of ability is **gifted**. She had a lot of running ability, so she was a **gifted** runner.
   - He had a lot of speaking ability, so he _____.

5. **wisdom**—**Great knowledge** is **wisdom.**
   - If a person has great knowledge, that person has _____.

PART C   Story Items

1. Two boys were born on the same day.
   a. In what year were they born?
   b. In what year were they ten years old?
   c. That was more than _____ years ago.
   d. In which city were they born?
      - Liverpool   • Chicago
      - London
   e. In which country were they born?
      - England   • United States

2. a. What was the full name of the boy whose family wanted him so much?
   b. Why did everybody want that boy so much?
   c. What was the full name of the boy whose family did not want him?
   d. Why didn't that boy's family want him?

3. a. How many years did Tom go to school?
   b. How did he get money for his family?
   c. Write the name of the lane that Tom's family lived on.
   d. How many rooms did his family have?
   e. Where did Tom sleep?
   f. What did he cover himself with at night?
   g. Name Tom's sisters.
   h. Much of the time, Tom was _____.
      - hungry   • not hungry
   i. Name **two** skills Tom had that impressed people he knew.

   j. What kind of person did Tom desire to see?

4. Tom found some old books.
   a. What kind of people were the books about?
   b. What kind of person did Tom begin to imitate?
   c. Tom's friends began to treat him with great _____.
      - anger   • respect   • joy
   d. Why did adults bring their problems to Tom?
   e. Tom became a hero to all who knew him, except for one group of people. Who were those people?

5. One day, Tom went out walking.
   a. How old was Tom at that time?
   b. How old were his sisters at that time?
   c. How was he trying to make money?
   d. What did he have on his feet?
   e. How often had he eaten pork pies?

6. The next day, Tom went out walking again.
   a. Did he know where he was going?
   b. Name the splendid place he came to.
   c. Which king lived in that palace?
   d. Which royal person did Tom see on the other side of the gate?
   e. What weapon did that person have at his side?
   f. Why did Tom come closer to the gate?
   g. Who grabbed Tom?
   h. Who became angry with the person who grabbed Tom?

PART D　Review Items

7. Use the words in the box to fill in the blanks or replace the underlined word.

confined	humble
ruler	wages
a little fat	rumor
plague	scampered
interested and delighted	abandon

a. Hal would not stop reading the book because it <u>fascinated</u> him so much.

b. As it began to rain, the dogs <u>scurried</u> for shelter.

c. The well fed puppies were round and <u>plump</u>.

d. The long storm made her _____ her plan to leave the village.

e. They _____ the goat to the pasture.

f. Despite her great wealth, the princess was a _____ person.

PART E　Writing Assignment

Would you want to be a prince or a princess?

Write at least **five** sentences that explain your answer.

Lesson 99

PART A　Word Lists

1	2	3	4	5
			Vocabulary review	**New vocabulary**
salute	gifted	entertain	1. ability	1. rude
hustle	feasted	entertainment	2. wisdom	2. salute
dignity	dilapidated	wrestle	3. unleash	3. priest
alley	enchanted	bruise	4. ignorant	4. trade
	drifted	shove	5. gifted	5. tattered
	suspected	wrestling		6. hustle

PART B　New Vocabulary

1. rude—The opposite of **polite** is **rude.** The opposite of a **polite** party is a **rude** party.
　a. What's the opposite of a **polite** student?
　b. What's the opposite of a **polite** experience?

2. salute—When you **salute,** you make a gesture that shows respect.
　● Show how soliders **salute** officers.

3. priest—A **priest** is an important man who works in a church. When you talk to a **priest**, you call him, "Father."

4. trade—What do you do when you **trade** with another person?

5. tattered—Something that is torn and shredded is called **tattered.** A torn and shredded coat is a **tattered** coat.
　● A torn and shredded shirt is _____.

6. hustle—When you move very fast, you **hustle.**
　● What are you doing when you move very fast?

PART C   Story Items

1. **a.** At the beginning of the chapter, what did Edward tell the guard to do?
   b. How did Edward think that Tom had been treated?
   c. The lords objected to what Edward had done. Why did they object?
   d. How did Edward quiet the lords?

2. Edward asked Tom how he spent his days.
   a. How did Tom's answers make Edward feel?
      ● happy   ● envious   ● tired
   b. Edward was surprised that Tom's sisters got dressed without help. Who did Edward think should help them?
   c. Why did Tom say that his sisters needed only one set of clothes?
   d. Did Edward think that Tom had a great deal of schooling?
   e. Why did Edward think that?
   f. Tom explained what he did for entertainment. Name at least **three** things he did.
   g. Was Edward permitted to do any of those things?

3. **a.** Edward wanted experiences like the ones _____ had.
   b. Tom wanted experiences like the ones _____ had.
   c. What did the two boys decide to do?

4. **a.** What did the boys discover when they stood in front of the mirror?
   b. What was the only difference in how they looked?
   c. Who had injured Tom?
   d. Who did Edward leave the room to go see?

5. **a.** What did Edward do with a strange object just before leaving the room?
   b. Who saw him do this?

6. **a.** When Edward arrived at the gate, how was he dressed?
   b. What did the guard do to Edward?
   c. How did the crowd treat Edward?

7. Before Tom and Edward met each other, they had different experiences in life. Write whether each statement describes **Tom** or **Edward**.
   a. He played tag in the river.
   b. He could wander through the city.
   c. He spent most of his time inside.
   d. He imagined that he was somebody else.
   e. He could not play with other boys.
   f. People helped him do almost everything.

PART D   Review Items

8. **Use the words in the box to fill in the blanks or replace the underlined words.**

optimistic	wisdom	distressed
great sorrow	unleash	plague
opportunity	baby	pauper

   a. Mary would often take care of her <u>infant</u> sister.
   b. Their fighting <u>troubled</u> her, and she begged them to stop.
   c. Lisa had an _____ to get a better job.
   d. Jerry was happy and _____ about starting his new career.
   e. The poor and hungry woman was a _____ .

PART E   Writing Assignment

Edward and Tom talked about how their lives were different. Which person would you want to be?

Write at least **five** sentences that explain your answer.

Lesson 100

PART A Word Lists

1	2	3	4
dirty	remodel	**Vocabulary review**	**New vocabulary**
sorry	whisk	1. salute	1. torment
poverty	remodeling	2. rude	2. sole
crazy	whisked	3. hustle	3. saucer
misery	merciful	4. tattered	4. dignity
mercy	sauce		5. alley
	saucer		6. foul
	sword		
	stricken		

PART B New Vocabulary

1. **torment**—The crowd teased and annoyed him so much that he could hardly stand the **torment.**
   - What does **torment** mean?

2. **sole**—A **sole** is the bottom part of your foot or of your shoes.
   - Touch the sole of your shoe.

3. **saucer**—A **saucer** is a little plate that is placed under a cup.
   - What do we call a little plate that is placed under a cup?

4. **dignity**—When somebody acts with confidence and good manners, that person acts with **dignity.**
   - The queen acted with confidence and good manners, so the queen acted with _____.

5. **alley**
   - What is an **alley?**

6. **foul**—Another word for **very bad** is **foul.**
   A very bad sight is a **foul** sight.
   - A very bad smell is a _____.

PART C Story Items

1. Edward was outside the gates.
   a. What did he say that made the crowd tease him?
   b. What did Edward finally do so that the crowd would stop teasing him?
   c. Why was he so unfamiliar with the city?
   d. Why were his feet so sore?
   e. What building did Edward finally recognize?
   f. Edward thought he would get help there because his father _____.
      - had taken over the building
      - lived in the building

2. Edward met some boys.
   a. Their haircuts looked as if a _____ had been placed over their heads.
   b. Who did Edward ask to speak to at the church?
      - John Canty
      - The schoolmaster
      - the priest
   c. How did the boys treat Edward when he demanded to see that person?
   d. What did Edward reach for on his hip?
   e. Why did his action make the boys laugh again?
   f. What did the boys finally do to Edward?

3. Edward came up with a plan to find somebody else who could help him.
   a. Who did Edward decide to go see?
   b. Where did Edward want those people to take him?
   c. Which person grabbed Edward by the collar?
   d. Who did that person think Edward was?
   e. Was that person mad at Edward?
4. Edward was dragged into a room.
   a. What material did Edward see on the floor?
   b. Edward thought he was having a

   _____.
   - daydream   - nightmare
   - a pleasant experience

PART D   Review Items

5. **Use the words in the box to fill in the blanks or replace the underlined words.**

walk over	confined
filth	vigorous
ignorant	pauper
humble	scurried
wisdom	gifted
ability	optimistic

   a. Once the girl recovered from her illness, she felt healthy and lively.

   b. During most of the day, the prisoners were _____ to their cells.
   c. Michi was not skeptical, but very _____ about the new plan.
   d. He could not read and he was _____ about history.
   e. Mary never had the _____ to swim.
   f. The hungry mice scampered around in their search for food.
   g. Her parents said that her talent would make her a _____ artist.
   h. After she had graduated from college, she felt that she had a lot of great knowledge.
   i. Although the queen had done many great deeds, she remained a _____ person.

PART E   Writing Assignment

Edward is having a hard time convincing people that he is the real prince.

What do you think he should do to convince people?

Write at least **five** sentences that explain your answer.

Lesson 101

PART A   Word Lists

1	2	3	4
poverty	pose	**Vocabulary review**	**New vocabulary**
alley	magnificent	1. saucer	1. regain your senses
crazy	magnificence	2. foul	2. pose
misery	activity	3. torment	3. merciful
dignity	activities	4. sole	4. stricken
	posing	5. dignity	

PART B   New Vocabulary

1. **regain your senses**—If you lose the power to think clearly, you lose your senses.
   - If you **regain** the power to think clearly, you _____.

2. **pose**—When you **pose**, you try to look very attractive. A boy who is trying to look very attractive in front of a girl is **posing** in front of a girl.
   - A boy who is trying to look very attractive in front of a mirror is _____.

3. **merciful**—The opposite of **cruel** is **merciful.**
   a. What's the opposite of a **cruel king?**
   b. What's the opposite of a **cruel act?**

4. **stricken**—When you are struck by a powerful emotion, you are **stricken** by that emotion. If you are struck by horror, you are horror-stricken.
   - If you are struck by grief, you are _____.

PART C   Story Items

1. a. Where was Tom Canty in this part of the story?
   b. Whose clothes was Tom wearing?
   c. Who did Tom pretend to act like?
   d. How did Tom feel when he realized that Edward wasn't coming back?
   e. What did Tom think would happen to him if somebody caught him?
2. a. Write the name of the young girl who came into the room.
   b. What did Tom do when he saw that girl?
   c. Why was Tom's action so shocking to her?
   d. What did she think was wrong with the prince?
3. Tom was led to an important man.
   a. Who was that man?
   b. What did that man look like?
   c. Who did that man think Tom was?
   d. What did Tom think was going to happen to him?
   e. What did the man say that made Tom so happy?
   f. Where did Tom ask to go?
4. The king asked Tom some questions.
   a. The king hoped that the questions would prove that Tom was

   _____.

   - crazy   • not crazy   • sick
   b. Which question did Tom answer correctly?
   c. Why do you think Tom got that answer right?
   d. Which question couldn't Tom answer?
   e. Why couldn't Tom answer that question?
   f. What did the king think had caused Tom's problem?
   - too much play
   - too much sleep
   - too much studying

g. What did the king think might solve Tom's problem?
- less studying
- less sleep
- more studying

5. Tom went back to Edward's room.
   a. Where did Tom long to be?
   b. Tom found out that a prince's life is very _____.
   - wonderful
   - dreary
   - happy

PART D   Review Items

6. **Use the words in the box to fill in the blanks or replace the underlined words.**

spectacular	donate
rude	ability
gloomy	abandoned
vigorous	baby
chance	plump

   a. Whenever she had the <u>opportunity</u> to go to the pool, she went swimming.

b. Joe was the only one who had enough _____ to sing the high notes.
c. The berries were <u>a little fat</u> and juicy.
d. They were tired after they completed the <u>lively</u> dance.
e. When the work got too hard she _____ her duties.
f. The view from the top of the mountain was <u>very impressive</u>.
g. Maria was insulted because the people had been _____ to her.

PART E   Writing Assignment

Tom is having a hard time convincing people that he is not the prince. What do you think he should do to convince them?

Write at least **five** sentences that explain your answer.

Lesson 102

PART A   Word Lists

1	2	3
identical	Elizabeth	**New vocabulary**
Hertford	hesitate	1. page
banquet	cause	2. dismiss
advantage	hesitating	3. mad
	causing	4. identical
	hesitant	

PART B   New Vocabulary

1. **page**—A **page** is a young boy who serves a member of a royal family.
   - What do we call a young boy who serves a member of a royal family?

2. **dismiss**—When you **dismiss** somebody, you tell that person to leave. If you tell a servant to leave, you **dismiss** a servant.
   - What do you do if you tell a class to leave?

3. **mad**—**Mad** is another word for **insane.**
   a. What's another way of saying **She was insane?**
   b. What's another way of saying **The king was insane?**

4. **identical**—Things that are **identical** are the same in every way. Shoes that are the same in every way are **identical** shoes.
   - What are houses that are the same in every way?

PART C   Vocabulary Review

foul
stricken
pose
ability
regain your senses
abandon
merciful

1. a. The opposite of **cruel** is
      _____ .

   b. What's the opposite of a **cruel act**?
      _____

   c. What's the opposite of a **cruel king**?
      _____

2. a. When you are struck by a powerful
      emotion, you are _____ by
      that emotion.

   b. If you are struck by horror, you are
      _____ .

   c. If you are struck by grief, you are
      _____ .

3. If you regain the power to think clearly,
   you _____ .

4. a. When you try to look very
      attractive, you _____ .

   b. A boy who is trying to look very
      attractive in front of a girl is
      _____ .

   c. A child who is trying to look very
      attractive in front of a mirror is
      _____ .

PART D   Story Items

1. a. What was the name of Tom's
      teacher?
   b. What event was Tom supposed to
      attend?
   c. When was that event going to occur?
2. Two young girls came to see Tom.
   a. Which girl had Tom already met?
   b. What was the other girl's name?
   c. Hertford told Tom to pretend that
      his memory was _____ .
3. a. What happened when Tom touched
      the water pitcher?
   b. What were the servants waiting for
      as they stood near Tom?
4. Hertford talked to another man.
   a. What was that man's name?
   b. What did that man think would soon
      happen to the king?
   c. Who would become king then?
   d. How did that possibility make the
      man feel?
      ● proud   ● nervous   ● pleased
   e. Hertford thought that the prince had
      changed in many ways. Name at
      least **two** ways.

5. a. At first, Hertford guessed that Tom
      was _____ .
      ● the real prince
      ● the prince's twin
   b. Was his guess correct?
   c. Did Hertford think his guess was
      correct?
   d. Finally, Hertford concluded that
      Tom was _____ .
      ● the real prince
      ● the prince's twin
6. Tom did some things that made people
   think the prince was crazy. Below is a
   list of things that Tom might do.
   Write **normal** if people would think it is
   normal for the prince to do.
   Write **crazy** if people would think it is
   crazy for the prince to do.
   a. Know about upcoming events.
   b. Tell a servant to cut his food for him.
   c. Call Lady Jane his sister.
   d. Say that his father was a thief.
   e. Know how to make his servants go
      away.
   f. Know how to speak French.

PART E   Review Items

7. **Use the words in the box to fill in the blanks or replace the underlined words.**

pauper	torn and shredded
optimistic	gifted
hustled	plague
torment	ignorant
ability	infant
confined	

a. She felt _____ that wonderful things would happen.

b. After the accident, she was _____ to a wheelchair for the rest of her life.

c. Steven did not have very much money, but he was not a _____.

d. Leslie had never learned how to drive and was _____ about cars.

e. He was not _____ enough to win the art contest.

f. The beggar wore a suit of <u>tattered</u> rags.

g. The frightened girl _____ out of the haunted house.

h. The prisoner could not stand the _____ of having only bread and water for her meals.

PART F   Writing Assignment

Pretend you are Henry the Eighth.

Write at least **five** sentences that describe the thoughts you are having about your son Edward.

Lesson 103

PART A   Word Lists

1
sternly
gently
gracefully
pleasantly
hesitantly

2
New vocabulary
1. take advantage
2. lumbering
3. stout
4. retreat
5. seaman

PART B   New Vocabulary

1. **take advantage**—When a person is helpless and you make that person do what you want, you **take advantage** of that person.
   - How could a boss take advantage of a very poor person?

2. **lumbering**—When you walk with very heavy steps, you are **lumbering.**
   - What are you doing when you walk with very heavy steps?

3. **stout**—Something that is very thick and sturdy is called **stout.** A thick and sturdy stick is a **stout** stick.
   - What's a thick and sturdy person?

4. **retreat**—When you **retreat,** you move backwards.
   a. What's another way of saying **He moved backwards toward the door?**
   b. What's another way of saying **She could not move backwards any farther?**

5. **seaman**—Another word for a **sailor** is a **seaman.**
   a. What's another way of saying **The sailor was stout?**
   b. What's another way of saying **Ten sailors lumbered down the street?**

PART C   Vocabulary Review

identical
tattered
ignorant
a page
dismiss
mad
optimistic

1. A young boy who serves a member of the royal family is called _____ .

2. **a.** When you tell people to leave, you _____ them.

   b. If you tell a class to leave, you _____ .

   c. If you tell a servant to leave, you _____ .

3. **a.** Things that are the same in every way are _____ things.

   b. Shoes that are the same in every way are _____ .

   c. Houses that are the same in every way are _____ .

4. **a.** Another word for **insane** is _____ .

   b. What's another way of saying **She was insane?** _____

   c. What's another way of saying **The king was insane?** _____

PART D   Story Items

1. **a.** Where was Edward when he woke up?

   b. What did Tom's father think that Edward should have brought home?

   c. Who felt sorry for Edward?

   d. What did Tom's mother think had ruined Edward's mind?

   e. What did Tom's sisters think Edward should do?

   f. Tom's father took Edward with him to get money for _____ .

2. Tom's mother thought about something unusual that Edward had done during the night. What had he done?

3. Edward and John Canty went into the street.

   a. Who came lumbering toward them?

   b. Why was that person looking for John Canty?

   c. What did John Canty do as the man approached?

   d. Where did John tell Edward to go in case they got separated?

   e. Who tried to slow John down?

   f. What did Edward do when that happened?

4. Edward formed a plan.

   a. What important event would occur that evening?

   b. Would Tom be present at that event?

   c. What did Edward plan to do when he got to the banquet?

   d. Was Edward's belief about Tom correct?

5. Tom's mother is not sure that Edward is her son. Below is a list of things that Edward might do.
   Write **both** after the things that both Tom and Edward would do.
   Write **only Edward** after the things that only Edward would do.

   a. Sleep on the floor.

   b. Cry out at night.

   c. Say he was the Prince of Wales.

   d. Read a book.

   e. Know how to speak French.

   f. Expect someone to dress him in the morning.

PART E   Review Items

6. Use the words in the box to fill in the blanks or replace the underlined words.

> tried to look very attractive
> scurried   rude
> ignorant   spectacular
> abandoned   dignity
> vigorous   foul
> confine

a. You shouldn't try to _____ a wild animal to a small cage.

b. She was outstanding at all sporting events, but she was the most impressive in the long jump.

c. Todd acted as if he knew everything, but he was really very _____.

d. The food was so very bad that they could not even swallow it.

e. Taka was so _____ to her neighbors that they did not like to have her in their house.

f. The people acted with confidence and good manners even though they did not agree with the king's speech.

g. The children posed as the photographers took their picture.

PART F   Writing Assignment

Pretend you are Tom's mother.

Write at least **five** sentences that describe the thoughts you are having about Edward.

Lesson 104

PART A   Word Lists

1	2	3
Thames River	merry	**New vocabulary**
wand	merriment	1. vast
cushion	hurl	2. barge
ragged	shield	3. file
suspicious	hurled	4. wand
ruffian		

PART B   New Vocabulary

1. vast—Something that is **very large** is **vast.**
  a. What's a **very large** room?
  b. What's a **very large** river?

2. barge—A **barge** is a large, flat boat that can carry cargoes on rivers. State barges are **barges** that are owned by the state.
  a. What do we call flat boats that can carry cargoes on rivers?
  b. What do we call those boats when they are owned by the state?

3. file—A **file** is a line. A line of people is a **file** of people.
  ● What is a line of barges?

4. wand—A **wand** is a small staff that is decorated.
  ● What do we call a small staff that is decorated?

PART C   Vocabulary Review

rude
lumbering
seaman
dignity
take advantage
retreat
ignorant
stout

1. When someone is helpless and you make that person do what you want, you _____ of that person.

2. a. Another word for a **sailor** is a _____.

   b. What's another way of saying **Ten sailors ran down the street?** _____

   c. What's another way of saying **The sailor was tall?** _____

3. a. Something that is very thick and sturdy is called _____.

   b. A thick and sturdy stick is a _____.

   c. A thick and sturdy person is a _____.

4. a. When you move backwards, you _____.

   b. What's another way of saying **He moved backwards toward the door?** _____

   c. What's another way of saying **She could not move backwards any farther?** _____

5. When you walk with very heavy steps, you are _____.

PART D   Story Items

1. a. What time of day was it when the royal party left the palace?
   b. Name the river they traveled on.
   c. Was the river bright or dark?
   d. What was the river crowded with?
   e. Name at least **three** decorations the boats had.
   f. Where was the royal family going?

2. a. In which city was the banquet hall?
   b. In which part of the banquet hall did the family sit?
      • In the rear
      • In the front
      • In the middle
   c. What did the people do when Tom stood up?
   d. What did Tom do to signal the start of the banquet?

3. a. Who was outside the hall trying to get past the gates?
   b. Who did that person say he was?
   c. How did the crowd respond to that person?
   d. Who came forward to help Edward?
   e. What did that man pull out when a seaman touched Edward?

   f. Who did the crowd start to move toward?
   g. The crowd stopped when _____ went by.
      • the king's messenger
      • the king
      • the Prince of Wales
   h. When that person went by, what did Miles and Edward do?

4. a. What message did the messenger bring?
   b. What phrase did the people shout when they heard that message?
   c. Who was the new king?
   d. Who should have been the new king?

PART E   Review Items

5. **Use the words in the box to fill in the blanks.**

tattered	wisdom	foul
merciful	chance	rude
abandoned	infant	torment

   a. When they showed her that the plan would not work, she _____ the idea.

b. All the people turned to him, because he had more _____ than any of the other rulers.

c. Their yard was filthy and in the corner was a pile of _____ garbage.

d. He was so ill-mannered and _____ that he didn't even thank her for being kind to him.

e. Leslie's skirt was old and _____ .

f. The stinging bees gave the yelping puppy a great deal of _____ .

g. The prisoners knew that the _____ ruler would set them free.

PART F   Writing Assignment

Tom could now make any command he wanted. Why do you think he didn't command someone to find Edward?

Write at least **five** sentences that explain your answer.

Lesson 105

PART A   Word Lists

1	2	3
blurred	swallow	**New vocabulary**
curse	basin	1. shudder
injury	faults	2. blurred
return	swallowed	3. inn
		4. regret
		5. belongings
		6. convince

PART B   New Vocabulary

1. **shudder**—Another word for **shiver** is **shudder.**
   a. Show how you shudder.
   b. What did you just do?

2. **blurred**—Things that do not look clear are **blurred.** A picture that does not look clear is a blurred picture.
   ● What is an image that does not look clear?

3. **inn**—An **inn** is a small hotel that serves meals and has rooms for people to stay.
   ● What's another word for a small hotel?

4. **regret**—When you are very sorry about something that happened, you **regret** that thing.
   a. What's another way of saying **She was sorry about what she had done?**

   b. What's another way of saying **She would not be sorry about what she did?**

5. **belongings**—The things that you own are your **belongings.**
   ● What do we call the things that we own?

6. **convince**—When you make somebody believe something, you convince that person it is true.
   a. What's another way of saying **She made her mother believe that she worked hard?**
   b. What's another way of saying **He will try to make me believe that it is true?**

PART C Vocabulary Review

```
barge
wisdom
wand
merciful
foul
vast
file
```

1. a. Something that is very large is
   _____ .

   b. A very large room is a _____ .
   c. A very large river is a _____ .

2. A large, flat boat that can carry cargoes on rivers is called a _____ .
3. a. A line is a _____ .
   b. A line of people is a _____ .
   c. A line of barges is a _____ .
4. A small staff that is decorated is called a
   _____ .

PART D Story Items

1. a. Where were Edward and Miles going at the beginning of this chapter?
   - To London Bridge
   - To Pudding Lane
   - To Miles's palace

   b. Edward heard some news about Henry the Eighth that made him sad. What was the news?
   c. What was Edward's new title?

2. a. Miles lived in _____ .
   - a palace • a house • an inn

   b. Where was that place?
   c. Who was waiting for Edward on the bridge?
   d. What did that person want to do with Edward?

3. a. Did Miles believe that Edward was really the king?
   b. Why did Miles admire Edward?
   c. What did Edward expect Miles to do with the towel?
   d. Why did Edward expect Miles to obey him?

4. Miles told his story.
   a. Was Miles's father a nobleman?
   b. Who had convinced Miles's father to throw Miles out?
   c. Where had Miles been for seven years?
   d. Did Miles have much money?

5. Edward told his story.
   a. Did Miles believe Edward's story?
   b. Miles resolved to take care of Edward until his mind _____ .
   c. Edward told Miles to kneel. Then he made Miles a _____ .
   d. What was Miles's new name?
   e. What could Miles and members of his family do?

PART E Review Items

6. **Use the words in the box to fill in the blanks or replace the underlined words.**

```
confidence and good manners
very impressive
move very fast       donate
take advantage       gifted
lanterns             barge
lumbering            rude
filthy               file
vast                 stout
retreat              wand
```

   a. When you move backwards, you
      _____ .

   b. When someone is helpless and you make that person do what you want, you _____ of that person.

c. Lamps that burn oil or candles are called _____.

d. A line is a _____.

e. Another word for **very large** is _____.

f. The old gentleman always acted with dignity.

g. The Linns had to hustle so they would not be late for the party.

h. The whole family was very polite except for Judy, who was very _____.

i. His supervisor praised him for the spectacular job that he had done.

j. A large, flat boat that can carry cargoes on rivers is called a _____.

k. A small staff that is decorated is called a _____.

l. When you walk with very heavy steps, you are _____.

m. Something that is very thick and sturdy is _____.

PART F   Writing Assignment

Miles has some doubts about Edward's story. Pretend you are Miles.

Write at least **five** sentences that describe what you think of Edward's story.

Lesson 106

PART A   Word Lists

1
innkeeper
hardship
madman
grandmother

2
plunge
worm
busy
busied
wormed
yawn
plunged

3
1. ruffian
2. suspicious
3. drowsy

PART B   New Vocabulary

1. ruffian—A **ruffian** is a rude and rough person.
● What's another word for a **rude and rough person?**

2. suspicious—When you are **suspicious** about something, you don't really believe that it is true. If you don't really believe a statement, you are **suspicious** about that statement.
● If you don't really believe a person, _____.

3. drowsy—It was very late at night and she was so **drowsy** she could hardly keep her eyes open.
● What could **drowsy** mean?

PART C   Vocabulary Review

> lantern
> inn
> shudder
> donate
> belongings
> convince
> regret
> hustle
> blurred

1. The things that you own are your _____.

2. a. Things that do not look clear are _____.

   b. A picture that does not look clear is a _____.

   c. An image that does not look clear is a _____.

3. Another word for a **small hotel** that serves meals and has rooms for people to stay is an _____.

4. a. When you are very sorry about something that happened, you _____ that thing.

   b. What's another way of saying **She was sorry about what she had done?** _____

   c. What's another way of saying **She would not be sorry about what she did?** _____

5. Another word for **shiver** is _____.

6. a. When you make somebody believe something, you _____ that person it is true.

   b. What's another way of saying **He will try to make me believe that it is true?** _____

   c. What's another way of saying **She made her mother believe that she worked hard?** _____

PART D   Story Items

1. Miles and Edward got ready for bed.
   a. Where did Edward tell Miles to sleep?
   b. Why did Edward want Miles to sleep in that spot?

2. a. When Miles woke up, what did he decide to mend?
   b. Why did Miles decide to leave?
   c. How long was Miles gone?
   d. When he returned, who did Miles think was under the bed covers?
   e. What was really under the bed covers?

3. a. Who did Miles call for after he pulled back the covers?
   b. That person told Miles that _____ had come into the room.
   c. The person who came to the room said he had a _____ from Miles.
   d. Who followed Edward and the boy after they left the inn?

4. Miles left the inn.
   a. Who was he looking for?
   b. Did Miles know where to look?
   c. Explain why Miles was so determined to find that person.

5. Here is a list of events from this chapter:
   - A messenger came to see Edward.
   - Edward went to sleep.
   - Miles left the inn to buy a needle and thread.
   - Miles left the inn to find Edward.
   a. Write the event that occurred **first?**
   b. Write the event that occurred **last.**

PART E   Review Items

6. Use the words in the box to fill in the blanks.

belongings	posed	inn
ignorant	vast	convince
ability	donate	shudder
regret	merciful	scamper
blurred		

a. The child was not stupid; she was just _____.

b. The girl _____ in front of the mirror.

c. Judy was always kind and _____ to the paupers.

d. When you make somebody believe something, you _____ that person it is true.

e. Another word for **shiver** is _____.

f. The things that you own are your _____.

g. Another word for a **small hotel** that serves meals and has rooms for people to stay is an _____.

h. When you are sorry about something that happened, you _____ that thing.

i. Things that do not look clear are _____.

j. Another word for **very large** is _____.

PART F   Writing Assignment

Miles will have a hard time finding Edward.

Write at least **five** sentences that explain what you think Miles should do.

Lesson 107

PART A   Word Lists

1	2	3
mourn	background	**New vocabulary**
secretary	daylight	1. article of clothing
Humphry	hairdresser	2. garment
parlor	fingernails	3. ordeal
	withdrawn	4. mourn
	ordeal	5. shattered
		6. withdraw
		7. assist
		8. parlor

PART B   New Vocabulary

1. **article of clothing**—An **article of clothing** is a piece of clothing.

2. **garment**—Another word for an **article of clothing** is a **garment.**

3. **ordeal**—An extremely difficult experience is an **ordeal.**
   - What's another way of saying **She suffered through an extremely difficult experience?**

4. **mourn**—When you **mourn** the death of a person, you show that you are very sad about that person's death.

5. **shattered**—When something is broken into many pieces, it is **shattered.** A window that is broken into many pieces is a **shattered** window.
   - What is a hope that is broken into many pieces?

6. **withdraw**—When you take something back, you **withdraw** that thing. When you take back your hand, you **withdraw** your hand.
   - When you take back a suggestion, you _____.

7. **assist**—When you help somebody, you **assist** that person.

8. **parlor**—A **living room** or a **small sitting room** is a **parlor.**
   - What's a living room or a small sitting room?

PART C   Vocabulary Review

```
merciful
regret
ruffian
drowsy
shudder
suspicious
```

1. It was very late at night and she was so _____ she could hardly keep her eyes open.

2. A person who is rude and rough is called a _____.

3. a. When you don't really believe that something is true, you are _____ about that thing.
   b. If you don't really believe a statement, you are _____.
   c. If you don't really believe a person _____.

PART D   Story Items

1. a. Where was Tom when he woke up?
   b. Who was Tom tempted to call out to?
   c. What material did he think he would feel with his hand?
   d. What material did he actually feel with his hand?

2. Tom had a pleasant dream.
   a. What objects did he find in his dream?
   b. What did he decide to do with those objects?
   c. Why did his mother hug him in his dream?
   d. The dream showed that Tom wanted to go _____.
   e. Who shattered Tom's dream?

3. a. How many people dressed Tom?
   b. What was wrong with one of the socks?
   c. Where did that gentleman want to send the keeper of the socks?
   d. Did Tom agree?

4. a. What room did Tom go to, so he could conduct important business?
   b. Which person stood next to him?
   c. Why did Tom think that the court should move into a smaller place?
   d. What place did Tom start to recommend?
   e. Who signaled to Tom to stop talking?
   f. Why did the business in the throne room suddenly stop?

5. a. What was the name of the boy who came to Tom's apartment?
   b. What would happen to that boy when Tom made a mistake?
   c. How did Tom feel about that?
   d. What kind of information did Tom want from the whipping boy?

6. Tom was a different king than Henry the Eighth had been. Write whether **Tom** or **Henry the Eighth** might have said each thing.
   a. "I will punish anybody who speaks against me."
   b. "We have to start saving money."
   c. "I want to wear the finest clothes."
   d. "I will treat my subjects fairly."
   e. "I want as much power as I can get."

PART E   Review Items

7. **Use the words in the box to fill in the blanks.**

```
identical      blurred      mend
suspicious     convince     inn
belongings     dismiss      shudder
ruffian        posed        regret
```

   a. When you fix something, you _____ it.
   b. When you tell a person to leave, you _____ that person.
   c. Things that are the same in every way are _____.

d. When you make somebody believe something, you _____ that person it is true.

e. Another word for **shiver** is _____.

f. The things that you own are your _____.

g. When you don't really believe that something is true, you are _____ about that thing.

h. Things that do not look clear are _____.

i. When you are sorry about something that happened, you _____ that thing.

j. Another word for a **small hotel** that serves meals and has rooms for people to stay is an _____.

k. A rough and rude person is a _____.

PART F   Writing Assignment

Tom is now the King of England.

Write at least **five** commands that Tom could give to improve life in England.

Lesson 108

PART A   Word Lists

1
official
lawyer
Hugo
charred

2
New vocabulary
1. conduct business
2. official
3. seal
4. evidence
5. misplaced

PART B   New Vocabulary

1. **conduct business**—When you do business, you **conduct business.**

2. **official**—Rules are **official** if they come from an office that can make the rules.
   - A rule coming from the office of the President is an **official** rule. A rule coming from a court of law is an **official** rule.

3. **seal**—A **seal** is a tool that puts a special design on a piece of paper. The official papers that a king wrote always had a special design on them. That design was made by the royal **seal.** Unless a paper had that design, it was not official.

4. **evidence**—Facts that make you conclude something are **evidence.**
   - What **evidence** would make you conclude that somebody had walked through fresh snow?

5. **misplaced**—If you don't remember where you put something, you have **misplaced** that thing.
   - If you don't remember where you put your shoes, you have **misplaced** your shoes.
   - If you don't remember where you put your keys, you have _____.

PART C   Vocabulary Review

ordeal	mourn
parlor	identical
mend	shattered
garment	withdraw
assist	article of clothing
convince	

1. When you show that you are very sad about a person's death, you _____ the death of that person.
2. When you help somebody, you _____ that person.
3. a. An extremely difficult experience is an _____.
   b. What's another way of saying **She suffered through an extremely difficult experience?**
   _____

4. Another word for an **article of clothing** is a _____.
5. A **living room** or a **small sitting room** is a _____.
6. A piece of clothing is an _____.
7. a. When you take something back, you _____ that thing.
   b. When you take back your hand you _____ your hand.
   c. When you take back a suggestion, you _____.
8. a. When something is broken into many pieces, it is _____.
   b. A window that is broken into many pieces is a _____.
   c. A hope that is broken into many pieces is a _____.

PART D   Story Items

1. King Henry had a royal seal.
   a. What kind of papers was the seal used on?
   b. If a paper did not have the royal seal on it, it was not _____.
      • official   • magnificent
      • wealthy
   c. Who was trying to find the royal seal?
2. The sheriff brought three people before Tom.
   a. Who was the first person to come before Tom?
   b. Tom had seen that person do something that was very brave. What was that?
   c. What crime was the man charged with?
   d. Whose house had the man gone to?
   e. What happened shortly after the man left?
   f. Did the sheriff have any evidence that showed that the man would take somebody's life?
   g. What evidence showed that the man would take somebody's life?
   h. What did Tom finally do with the man?

3. a. Who was the next person to come before Tom?
   b. She was accused of being a _____.
   c. What was she accused of starting?
   d. How did the sheriff say she started it?
   e. Why did Tom ask the woman to take off her stockings?
   f. What happened when the woman took off her stockings?
   g. So what did Tom conclude about the woman's powers?
4. a. Who was the last person that came before Tom?
   b. How old was that person?
   c. Who was that person accused of making a contract with?
   d. Was that person English?
   e. What did the law say about English children and contracts?
   f. So what did Tom conclude about the contract that person had made?
   g. How did the lords react to Tom's decisions?

PART E   Review Items

5. **Use the words in the box to fill in the blanks.**

article of clothing	withdraw
suspicious	mend
take advantage	ruffian
identical	drowsy
shattered	mourn
retreat	blurred
ordeal	assist

a. When you move backwards, you
_____.

b. When you take something back, you
_____ that thing.

c. When you help somebody, you
_____ that person.

d. A piece of clothing is an _____.

e. When you don't really believe that
something is true, you are
_____ about that thing.

f. When you fix something, you
_____ it.

g. When something is broken into
many pieces, it is _____.

h. An extremely difficult experience is
an _____.

i. It was very late at night and she was
so _____ she could hardly
keep her eyes open.

j. When a person is helpless and you
make that person do what you want,
you _____ of that person.

k. When you show that you are very
sad about a person's death, you
_____ the death of that
person.

PART F   Writing Assignment

Write at least **five** sentences that
explain why Tom is starting to enjoy
being king.

Lesson 109

PART A   Word Lists

1
daylight
fingernails
innkeeper
background

2
New vocabulary
1. charred
2. sling

PART B   New Vocabulary

1. **charred**—Wood that has been badly
burned is **charred** wood.
   • Houses that are badly burned are
   _____.

2. **sling**—A **sling** is a loop of cloth that
you put your arm in when it is injured.
   • What do we call a loop of cloth that
   you put an injured arm in?

PART C   Vocabulary Review

> official
> evidence
> suspicious
> conduct business
> drowsy
> mourn
> seal
> misplaced

1. A tool that puts a special design on a piece of paper is a _____.
2. When you do business, you _____.
3. Facts that make you conclude something are _____.

4. a. If you don't remember where you put something, you have _____ that thing.
   b. If you don't remember where you put your shoes, you have _____.
   c. If you don't remember where you put your keys, you have _____.

5. a. If rules come from an office that can make the rules, the rules are _____.
   b. A rule coming from the office of the President is an _____ rule.
   c. A rule coming from a court of law is an _____.

PART D   Story Items

1. a. Who looked for Edward?
   b. Where did that person stop and eat supper?
   c. Where did Miles figure that Edward would go if he escaped?
   d. So where did Miles resolve to go?
2. a. Who had followed Edward and the boy on London Bridge?
   b. Why would it be hard to recognize that person?
   c. The boy told Edward that something had happened to Miles. What was that?
   d. What kind of building did the boy lead Edward into?
   e. What condition was that building in?
   f. Was Miles in the building?
   g. Who threatened to punish Edward?
   h. Who did that person think Edward was?
3. John Canty told Edward his problem.
   a. Who was he in trouble with?
   b. Why were they after him?
   c. Why had he changed his name?
   d. What was John Canty's new name?
   e. What was Edward's new name?
   f. What was the other boy's name?
4. a. How did Edward feel about his father?
   b. How did other people feel about Edward's father?

5. Edward went to sleep.
   a. What quiet sound did he hear when he woke up?
   b. What loud sound did he hear?
   c. What lit up the room?
   d. Describe at least **two** of the people who were in the room.
   e. What did Edward think of that scene?

PART E   Review Items

6. **Use the words in the box to fill in the blanks.**

> | conduct business | drowsy |
> | shattered | assist |
> | official | misplaced |
> | withdraw | ordeal |
> | vast | mourn |
> | evidence | seal |
> | garment | |

   a. When you show that you are very sad about a person's death, you _____ the death of that person.
   b. When you help somebody, you _____ that person.
   c. It was very late at night and she was so _____ she could hardly keep her eyes open.

d. A tool that puts a special design on a piece of paper is a _____ .

e. Facts that make you conclude something are _____ .

f. If rules come from an office that can make the rules, the rules are _____ .

g. If you don't remember where you put something, you have _____ that thing.

h. When something is broken into many pieces, it is _____ .

i. Another word for an **article of clothing** is a _____ .

j. When you do business, you _____ .

k. An extremely difficult experience is an _____ .

l. When you take something back, you _____ that thing.

m. Something that is very large is _____ .

PART F   Writing Assignment

Write at least **five** sentences that describe what you think Edward will do if he can escape from the gang.

Lesson 110

PART A   Word Lists

1	2	3	4	5
vagrant	eyesight	cross	**New vocabulary**	**New vocabulary**
capable	whirlwind	crisscross	1. capable of	6. vagrant
hurriedly	thundergust	string	2. brawl	7. burly
barrel	outskirts	stringy	3. brand	8. chant
	farmhouse	accident	4. prosper	9. limb
	clothesline	accidental	5. lash	
	overcast	accidentally		

PART B   New Vocabulary

1. **capable of**—If you are able to do something, you are **capable of** doing that thing. If you are able to swim, you are **capable of** swimming.
   a. If you are able to ride a horse, you are _____ .
   b. If you are able to read, you are _____ .

2. **brawl**—Another word for a **rough fight** is a **brawl**.
   ● What's another word for a **rough fight**?

3. **brand**—When you **brand** an animal, you take a hot iron and press it against the animal, so that it leaves a mark that won't go away.

4. **prosper**—When you **prosper**, you earn money and do well.
   ● What's another way of saying

She earned money and did well?

5. **lash**—Another word for **whip** is **lash**.
   ● What's another way of saying **The man whipped his horse?**

6. **vagrant**—A **vagrant** is a person who does not have any place to live and has no job.
   ● What do we call a person who does not have any place to live and has no job?

7. **burly**—Another word for **stout and strong** is **burly**.
   ● What's another way of saying **He was a stout and strong man?**

8. **chant**—When you say the same thing over and over, you **chant** that thing.

9. **limb**—A **limb** is an **arm** or a **leg**.
   ● What's an **arm** or a **leg**?
   ● What's another word for an **arm** or a **leg**?

PART C   Vocabulary Review

official
sling
evidence
garment
charred

1. **a.** Houses that are badly burned are
   _____ houses.
   b. Wood that has been badly burned is
   _____.

2. A loop of cloth that you put your arm in
   when it is injured is called a
   _____.

PART D   Story Items

1. When the gang started to make merry, a
   blind man did something that showed he
   was really a humbug.
   a. What did he do?
   b. A man with a wooden leg also
   showed that he was a humbug. What
   did he do?
2. **a.** What name was John Canty now
   using?
   b. Who was looking for Canty?
   c. Why were they after him?
   d. Where were the police more strict
   with the laws, in the country or in
   London?
3. **a.** What happened to a person if that
   person was caught begging for the
   first time?
   b. What happened if that person was
   caught a second time?
4. **a.** Who told the story about how he was
   branded and sold for a slave?
   b. What would happen to that man if
   he got caught again?
5. **a.** Who told the gang that the laws
   about begging would be changed?
   b. How did the gang respond to that
   announcement?
   c. Who became very angry with
   Edward for saying the things he
   said?
   d. Who prevented that person from
   getting his hands on Edward?
6. **a.** What new title did the gang make up
   for Edward?
   b. What did they robe him with?
   c. What did they use for his throne?
7. What did Edward do when a member of
   the gang tried to kiss his foot?

PART E   Review Items

8. Write which year each event took
   place in. Choose from **1889, 1893,
   1918,** or **1931.**
   a. World War One ends
   b. Jane Addams opens Hull House
   c. Jane Addams wins the Nobel Peace
   Prize
   d. A new factory law passes
9. Write which color each place was.
   a. Land of the Munchkins
   b. Emerald City
   c. Land of the Winkies
   d. Land of the Quadlings
10. **Use the words in the box to fill in the
    blanks.**

official	convince	evidence
parlor	regret	charred
sling	seal	assist

   a. When you make somebody believe
   something, you _____ that
   person it is true.
   b. Wood that has been badly burned is
   _____ wood.
   c. When you are sorry about
   something that happened, you
   _____ that thing.
   d. If rules come from an office that
   can make the rules, the rules are
   _____.
   e. A loop of cloth that you put an
   injured arm in is called a
   _____.
   f. Facts that make you conclude
   something are _____.
   g. The _____ was the fanciest
   room in the house.

PART F   Writing Assignment

Pretend you are one of the members of the gang.

Write at least **five** sentences that describe what your life is like.

Lesson 111

PART A   Word Lists

1	2	3
irritable	foolish	**New vocabulary**
hospitable	foolishness	1. run a risk
motley	assist	2. clothesline
	assistant	3. motley
		4. eye
		5. overcast
		6. hospitable
		7. irritable
		8. grope

PART B   New Vocabulary

1. **run a risk**—When you take a chance that may be dangerous, you **run a risk.**
   - What are you doing when you take a chance that may be dangerous?

2. **clothesline**—What is a **clothesline?**

3. **motley**—Something that is made up of many different types of things is called **motley.**
   - What kind of group is made up of many different kinds of people?

4. **eye**—When you **eye** something, you study it with your eyes. Here's another way of saying **She studied the painting with her eyes: She eyed the painting.**
   - What's another way of saying **He studied the jewels with his eyes?**

5. **overcast**—When the sky is gray and cloudy, the sky is **overcast.**
   - What's another way of saying **The day was gray and cloudy?**

6. **hospitable**—When you are **hospitable,** you show somebody hospitality.
   - A person who shows somebody hospitality is being _____.

7. **irritable**—When you are **irritable,** you are grouchy.
   - What's another way of saying **John Canty was grouchy?**

8. **grope**—When you feel your way in the dark, you **grope.**
   - What are you doing when you feel your way in the dark?

PART C   Vocabulary Review

prosper	limb
burly	vagrant
chant	convince
charred	lash
capable of	regret
brand	brawl

1. When you earn money and do well, you _____.

2. Another word for a **rough fight** is a _____.

3. Another word for an **arm** or a **leg** is _____.

4. When you take a hot iron and press it against an animal so that it leaves a mark that won't go away, you _____ that animal.

5. When you say the same thing over and over, you _____ that thing.

6. a. Another word for **whip** is _____.

   b. What's another way of saying **The man whipped his horse?** _____

7. a. Another word for **stout and strong** is _____.

   b. What's another way of saying **He was a stout and strong man?** _____

8. a. If you are able to do something, you are _____ doing that thing.

   b. If you are able to swim, you are _____.

   c. If you are able to read, you are _____.

   d. If you are able to ride a horse, you are _____.

9. A person who does not have any place to live and has no job is a _____.

PART D   Story Items

1. a. In the morning, what kind of mood were the vagrants in?
   b. What was the weather like?
2. How did the gang of vagrants greet strangers along the road?
3. a. Where did the gang have breakfast that morning?
   b. Name **two** terrible things the gang did at that place.
   c. The gang told the family who lived in that place that they would return if the family reported what happened. What did the gang say they would do when they returned?
4. a. Who did Edward go with when the gang reached a village?
   b. Why didn't that person steal anything in the village?
   c. When a stranger approached, what did Hugo do?
   d. What did Hugo ask for?
   e. The stranger said, "You shall have _____."
   f. Edward told the stranger how to make a miracle happen. What did Edward tell the stranger to do?

   g. What did Hugo do after Edward told the stranger about the miracle?
5. a. What did Edward do when Hugo left?
   b. How did the people treat Edward when he begged at farmhouses?
6. a. What time was it when Edward saw the lantern?
   b. The lantern was by the open door of a _____.
7. a. Who came into that building just after Edward entered it?
   b. Edward went to bed in a _____.
   c. What did Edward cover himself with?

PART E   Review Items

8. Use the words in the box to fill in the blanks.

vagrant	brand	official
prosper	sling	charred
burly	parlor	brawl
lash	limb	chant
regret	capable of	

a. Another word for a **rough fight** is a _____.

b. The people sat on the couch in the _____.

c. Another word for **stout and strong** is _____.

d. When you earn money and do well, you _____.

e. A person who does not have any place to live and has no job is a _____.

f. When you take a hot iron and press it against an animal so that it leaves a mark that won't go away, you _____ that animal.

g. When you say the same thing over and over, you _____ that thing.

h. Wood that has been badly burned is _____ wood.

i. If you are able to do something, you are _____ doing that thing.

j. Another word for **whip** is _____.

k. Another word for an **arm** or a **leg** is _____.

PART F   Writing Assignment

How do you think Hugo ended up with the gang? Make up a short biography of Hugo that explains why he joined the gang.

Make your biography at least **five** sentences.

Lesson 112

PART A   Word Lists

1	2	3
identify	rattle	**New vocabulary**
tragic	snuggle	1. gasp
calf	trouble	2. identify
weary	cattle	3. calf
gagged	terrible	4. widow
	hospitable	5. cattle
		6. weary
		7. tragic

PART B   New Vocabulary

1. **gasp**—Show me how you **gasp**.

2. **identify**—When you tell what something is, you **identify** that thing.
   a. When you tell the name of a tree, you _____.
   b. When you tell the name of an insect, you _____.

3. **calf**—A **calf** is a cow or a bull that is not full-grown.

4. **widow**—A **widow** is a woman whose husband is dead.

● What do we call a woman whose husband is dead?

5. **cattle**—Cows and bulls are **cattle**.

6. **weary**—Something that tires you, **wearies** you.
   a. What's another way of saying **The conversation tired her?**
   b. What's another way of saying **The work made her tired?**

7. **tragic**—Something that is very sad is **tragic**.
   a. A very sad accident is a _____.
   b. A very sad story is a _____.

PART C   Vocabulary Review

eye	irritable
overcast	burly
limb	motley
hospitable	run a risk
grope	brawl

1. a. When you are grouchy, you are
   _____.

   b. What's another way of saying
   John Canty was grouchy?
   _____

2. a. When the sky is cloudy and gray, the
   sky is _____.

   b. What's another way of saying
   The day was cloudy and gray?
   _____

3. Something that is made up of many
   different types of things is called
   _____.

4. When you feel your way in the dark,
   you _____.

5. a. When you study something with
   your eyes, you _____
   something.

   b. What's another way of saying
   **He studied the jewels with his
   eyes?** _____

6. When you show somebody hospitality,
   you are _____.

7. When you take a chance that may be
   dangerous, you _____.

PART D   Story Items

1. a. Where did Edward sleep that night?
   b. What was the weather like outside?
   c. What touched Edward when he was
   almost asleep?
   d. Why did Edward stretch his hand
   out?
   e. At first, what did Edward think that
   thing was?
   f. What did that thing turn out to be?
   g. So Edward put his blankets over
   himself and the _____.
   h. Edward felt _____ and
   comfortable.

2. a. Who came into the barn the next
   morning?
   b. What did Edward say that convinced
   the girls he was the king?
   c. The girls might not have believed
   Edward if they had been
   _____ and wiser.
   d. Why did the girls take Edward to
   their house?

3. The girls' mother talked to Edward.
   a. Did she believe that Edward was the
   king?
   b. Did she think that Edward was sane
   or crazy?
   c. Why did she talk about things that a
   king would not know about?
   d. Did Edward know about farm
   animals?

   e. What subject did Edward show
   interest in?
   f. Why do you think Edward showed
   interest?
   g. What job did the woman think that
   Edward had before?

4. To test Edward, the woman left the
   room.
   a. What was on the stove?
   b. The woman thought that Edward
   would _____ the hot cakes.
      ● take care of   ● ignore
   c. What did Edward do as the hot cakes
   burned?

5. a. Name **two** jobs the woman gave
   Edward after breakfast.
   b. When Edward was in the backyard,
   who approached the front gate?
   c. What did Edward do when he saw
   those people?

PART E   Review Items

6. Use the words in the box to fill in the blanks.

run a risk	charred	chant
hospitable	vagrant	eye
irritable	ordeal	grope
regret	brawl	limb
shattered	withdraw	burly
overcast	motley	convince
capable of	prosper	

a. When you take something back, you _____ that thing.

b. When something is broken into many pieces, it is _____.

c. Another word for a **rough fight** is a _____.

d. Another word for **stout and strong** is _____.

e. When you are grouchy, you are _____.

f. When you say the same thing over and over, you _____ that thing.

g. When the sky is cloudy and gray, the sky is _____.

h. An extremely difficult experience is an _____.

i. When you feel your way in the dark, you _____.

j. When you show somebody hospitality, you are _____.

k. When you earn money and do well, you _____.

l. Another word for an **arm** or a **leg** is _____.

m. If you are able to do something, you are _____ doing that thing.

n. A person who does not have any place to live and has no job is a _____.

o. When you take a chance that may be dangerous, you _____.

p. When you study something with your eyes, you _____ that thing.

q. Something that is made up of many different types of things is called _____.

PART F   Writing Assignment

The girls believed that Edward was the king. Would you have believed that Edward was the king?

Write at least **five** sentences that explain your answer.

Lesson 113

PART A Word Lists

1
tiptoes
fireplace
sheepskin
eyesight
clothesline

2
hospitable
comfortable
irritable
disagreeable

3
New vocabulary
1. tuck somebody into bed
2. bound and gagged
3. inform
4. intend
5. impulse
6. confess

PART B New Vocabulary

1. **tuck somebody into bed**—What do you do when you **tuck somebody into bed?**

2. **bound and gagged**—When a person is **bound,** that person is tied up. When a person is **gagged,** that person's mouth is covered and that person cannot talk.
   a. When a person is tied up, that person is _____.
   b. When a person's mouth is covered, that person is _____.

3. **inform**—When you give somebody information about something, you **inform** that person about that thing.
   a. What are you doing when you give a girl information about school?
   b. What are you doing when you give a man information about the weather?

4. **intend**—If you plan to do something, you **intend** to do that thing.
   a. A person who plans to go to a party, _____.
   b. A person who plans to stop at the inn, _____.

5. **impulse**—An **impulse** is a sudden, strong desire to do something.
   a. A person who has a sudden desire to eat has an _____.
   b. A person who has a sudden desire to run away has an _____.

6. **confess**—When somebody **confesses,** that person tells the truth about a secret.
   • What is a person doing when that person tells the truth about a secret?

PART C Vocabulary Review

wearies	motley
irritable	identify
widow	gasp
calf	prosper
tragic	cattle

1. A cow or a bull that is not full-grown is a _____.
2. a. When you tell what something is, you _____ that thing.
   b. When you tell the name of a person, you _____.
   c. When you tell the name of an insect, you _____.
   d. When you tell the name of a tree, you _____.
3. a. Something that is very sad is _____.
   b. A very sad story is a _____.
   c. A very sad accident is a _____.
4. a. Something that tires you, _____ you.
   b. What's another way of saying **The work made her tired?**
   c. What's another way of saying **The conversation tired her?**
5. Cows and bulls are _____.
6. A woman whose husband is dead is a _____.
7. Show me how you gasp.

PART D   Story Items

1. a. Edward followed the path from the farmhouse to a _____ .
   b. Who do you think was following him?
2. a. Edward saw a light coming from a _____ .
   b. Who lived in that place?
   c. Did that person believe that Edward was the king?
   d. The hermit told the king a secret. What was that secret?
3. a. What had Edward's father done to the hermit?
   b. Who did the hermit want to punish?
   c. What did the hermit do with Edward's ankles?
   d. What did he do with Edward's mouth?
   e. Which person made the hermit stop?
   f. Why couldn't Edward cry out to that person?
   g. What did the hermit throw over Edward?
   h. Who offered to show Miles where Edward was?
4. After Miles and the hermit had left, the door to the hut was opened.
   a. Who did Edward think opened the door?
   b. Was Edward afraid of that person?
   c. Who had really come into the hut?
   d. Why was Edward glad to see them?

PART E   Review Items

5. Use the words in the box to fill in the blanks.

irritable	calf	tragic
official	shattered	ordeal
identify	motley	weary
hospitable	cattle	widow

a. If rules come from an office that can make the rules, the rules are _____ .
b. A cow or a bull that is not full-grown is a _____ .
c. Something that is very sad is _____ .
d. A woman whose husband is dead is a _____ .
e. Something that is made up of many different types of things is called _____ .
f. Something that tires you, makes you feel _____ .
g. When you tell what something is, you _____ that thing.
h. Cows and bulls are _____ .
i. When you are grouchy, you are _____ .

PART F   Writing Assignment

Pretend you meet a person who says, "I am the King of England."

Write at least **five** questions you would ask that person to find out if he was telling the truth.

Lesson 114

PART A Word Lists

1
innocent
penalty
Edith
Arthur

2
troublesome
meantime
therefore
blacksmith
courtroom

3
situation
chuckle
suspicion
chuckling
gossip
daily

4
New vocabulary
1. band
2. mistreat
3. betray
4. innocent
5. flogged

PART B New Vocabulary

1. **band**—Another word for a **group** is a **band.**
   - A group of vagrants is a
   _____.

2. **mistreat**—When somebody is treated poorly, that person is **mistreated.**
   - If a dog is treated poorly, that dog is
   _____.

3. **betray**—You **betray** somebody by pretending to be that person's friend and then trick that person.
   - What are you doing to a person when you pretend to be a person's friend and then trick that person?

4. **innocent**—Someone who is not guilty of doing something wrong is **innocent.**
   - A person who is not guilty of cheating is _____.

5. **flogged**—When somebody is beaten with a whip or a switch, that person is **flogged.**

PART C Vocabulary Review

weary	intend	inform
bound	tragic	confesses
official	impulse	gagged

1. When a person tells the truth about a secret, that person _____ that secret.

2. a. When you give somebody information about something, you _____ that person about that thing.
   b. What are you doing when you give a man information about the weather? _____
   c. What are you doing when you give a girl information about school? _____

3. a. If you plan to do something, you _____ to do that thing.
   b. A person who plans to stop at the inn, _____.
   c. A person who plans to go to a party, _____.

4. a. A sudden, strong desire to do something is an _____.
   b. A person who suddenly has a very strong desire to run away has an _____.
   c. A person who suddenly has a very strong desire to eat has an _____.

5. a. When a person is tied up, that person is _____.
   b. When a person's mouth is covered, that person is _____.

PART D   Story Items

1. a. Which two thieves disliked Edward?
   b. What did Hugo "accidentally" do to make Edward angry?
   c. Which object did Edward use to defend himself?
   d. Why was Edward so skilled with that object?
2. Who wanted to turn Edward over to the law?
3. a. Who did Hugo run up to in the village?
   b. What object did he take from that person?
   c. Who did he give that object to?
   d. Who did the woman think had taken the object from her?
   e. What kind of man threatened Edward?
   f. Who stopped that person?
   g. How did he stop that person?
4. a. Who led Miles, the woman, and Edward away from the mob?
   b. Where did they go?
   c. What was in the woman's package?
   d. At first, the woman said the package was worth more than _____ pennies.
   e. If the package was worth more than _____ pennies, Edward would be _____.
   f. Then the woman said that the package was worth _____ pennies.
   g. Who stopped the woman in the hall and tried to buy her pig?
   h. Who heard that man talking to the woman?
   i. How much did the woman receive for the package?
5. What two punishments would Edward receive for his crime?

PART E   Review Items

6. **Use the words in the box to fill in the blanks.**

prosper	identify	eye
tragic	widow	inform
confesses	impulse	gagged
weary	gasp	intend
bound	grope	

   a. If you plan to do something, you _____ to do that thing.
   b. When somebody tells the truth about a secret, that person _____.
   c. Something that tires you, makes you feel _____.
   d. When a person has his mouth covered, that person is _____.
   e. Something that is very sad is _____.
   f. A sudden, strong desire to do something is an _____.
   g. When you tell what something is, you _____ that thing.
   h. When a person is tied up, that person is _____.
   i. A woman whose husband is dead is a _____.
   j. When you give somebody information about something, you _____ that person about that thing.

PART F   Writing Assignment

Edward is finding out what life is really like in England.

Write at least **three** things that Edward might change if he ever becomes king again.

Lesson 115

PART A   Word Lists

1
irritable
comfortable
hospitable
disagreeable

2
New vocabulary
1. duties
2. reel
3. bind
4. armed
5. penalty
6. slumber

PART B   New Vocabulary

1. **duties**—Your **duties** are the things that you must do. If a person must be at school on time, that person has a **duty** to be at school on time.
   - If a person must fix dinner, that person _____.

2. **reel**—Another word for **stagger** is **reel**. If a person **staggered** from a blow, that person **reeled** from the blow.
   - If the person staggered around the room, that person _____.

3. **bind**—If you **tie** somebody up, you **bind** that person. If you **tied** somebody up, you **bound** that person.
   a. What do you do if you **tie** somebody up?
   b. What did you do if you **tied** somebody up?

4. **armed**—Somebody who has a weapon is **armed**.

5. **penalty**—A **penalty** is the punishment somebody receives for breaking the rules.
   - What do we call the punishment somebody receives for breaking the rules?

6. **slumber**—Another word for **sleep** is **slumber**.
   a. What's another way of saying **He slept in the afternoon?**
   b. What's another way of saying **She slept for hours?**

PART C   Vocabulary Review

innocent	band
mistreated	bound
impulse	inform
flogged	betray

1. When somebody is beaten with a whip or a switch, that person is _____.
2. a. Someone who is not guilty of doing something wrong is _____.
   b. A person who is not guilty of stealing is _____.
   c. A person who is not guilty of cheating is _____.
3. a. Another word for a **group** is a _____.
   b. A group of vagrants is a _____.
4. a. When somebody is treated poorly, the person is _____.
   b. If a dog is treated poorly, that dog is _____.
5. When you pretend to be somebody's friend and then trick that person, you _____ that person.

PART D   Story Items

1. a. The officer led Miles and Edward to the _____ .
    b. What did Miles want the officer to do?
    c. What had the officer done that Miles knew about?
    d. Who did Miles threaten to tell his story to?
    e. What would have happened to the officer if the judge found out about his joke?
2. a. Where did Edward and Miles spend the night?
    b. Where did Edward and Miles go the next day?
    c. How many rooms did that place have?
    d. Why do you think Edward was not impressed by a place with so many rooms?
3. a. Who was the first person Miles and Edward met inside?
    b. Did that person say that he recognized Miles?
    c. Do you think that person actually recognized Miles?
    d. What did that person say had happened to Miles six years ago?
    e. What proof did that person have of that event?
    f. Which two relatives of Miles had died?
4. a. Who was the next person that Miles met?
    b. What were she and Miles going to do a long time ago?
    c. Did she say that she recognized Miles?
    d. What did Miles think that Hugh had done six years ago?
    e. Why would Hugh have done that?
    f. What did Hugh order the servants to do to Miles?
    g. Why didn't the servants do that?
5. Miles is having a hard time proving that he really is Miles Hendon. Here are some events.
    Write **yes** if the event might prove that Miles is telling the truth.
    Write **no** if the event might prove that

Miles is lying.
    a. Miles recognizes all the houses in his home village.
    b. Miles knows exactly how many rooms are in Hendon Hall.
    c. Hugh does not recognize Miles.
    d. A letter says that Miles is dead.
    e. Miles is able to show that Hugh is lying.

PART E   Review Items

6. Use the words in the box to fill in the blanks.

capable of	overcast	vagrant
intend	mistreated	motley
eye	impulse	prosper
innocent	flogged	band
inform	confesses	betray

    a. A person who does not have any place to live and has no job is a _____ .
    b. If you plan to do something, you _____ to do that thing.
    c. When you earn money and do well, you _____ .
    d. When you give somebody information about something, you _____ that person about that thing.
    e. When you pretend to be somebody's friend and then trick that person, you _____ that person.
    f. If you are able to do something, you are _____ doing that thing.
    g. When somebody tells the truth about a secret, that person _____ .
    h. A sudden, strong desire to do something is an _____ .
    i. Someone who is not guilty of doing something wrong is _____ .
    j. Another word for a **group** is a _____ .
    k. When somebody is treated poorly, that person is _____ .
    l. When somebody is beaten with a whip or a switch, that person is _____ .

PART F   Writing Assignment

Pretend you are Miles.

Write at least **five** sentences that explain what you would do to prove that you are really Miles Hendon.

Lesson 116

PART A   Word Lists

1
deny
coronation

2
overpowered
tormented
parted
remembered
horrified
treated

3
New vocabulary
1. prison cell
2. smuggle
3. deny
4. daily
5. stall
6. deathbeds
7. gossip
8. coronation

PART B   New Vocabulary

1. **prison cell**—A **prison cell** is a small room that prisoners live in.

2. **smuggle**—When you **smuggle** something, you hide it and take it to some place. If somebody hides some money and takes it into a prison cell, the person **smuggles** the money into the cell.

3. **deny**—When you say that something is not true, you **deny** that thing. When you say that you do not know a person, you **deny** knowing that person.
   - When you say you do not know a fact, you _____.

4. **daily**—Another word for **everyday** is **daily.**
   a. What's another way of saying **He ate everyday?**
   b. What's another way of saying **She visited her grandmother everyday?**

5. **stall**—When you **stall,** you try to put off doing something.
   - How could you **stall** if you were trying to put off going to the dentist?

6. **deathbeds**—People who are on their **deathbeds** are dying.

7. **gossip**—When you **gossip** about something, you tell rumors about that thing. When you tell rumors about a new person in school, you **gossip** about a new person in school.
   - When you tell rumors about something you don't like, you _____.

8. **coronation**—A **coronation** is an important event in which a crown is officially placed on the head of a new king. A new king is not officially a king until the **coronation.**

PART C   Vocabulary Review

bind	betray
slumber	bound
innocent	impulse
penalty	duties
armed	reel

1. The punishment somebody receives for breaking the rules is the _____.
2. If you tie somebody up, you _____ that person.
3. **a.** Another word for **stagger** is _____.
   b. If a person staggered from a blow, that person _____.
   c. If a person staggered around the room, that person _____.

4. **a.** Another word for **sleep** is _____.
   b. What's another way of saying **She slept for hours?** _____
   c. What's another way of saying **He slept in the afternoon?** _____

5. Somebody who has a weapon is _____.

6. **a.** The things that you should do are your _____.
   b. If a person should be at school on time, that person has a _____.
   c. If a person should fix dinner, that person has a _____.

7. If you tied somebody up, you _____ that person.

PART D   Story Items

1. **a.** What did Edward plan to write, so that he could prove that he was king?
   b. How many languages would he use?
2. **a.** Who was married to Hugh?
   b. Why did she tell Miles to leave?
   c. Why did Miles ask that person to look him in the eyes?
   d. Who entered the room and fought with Miles?
   e. Where did those people take Miles and Edward?
   f. How were Miles and Edward kept together?
3. An old man was brought into the prison cell.
   a. What was his name?
   b. Where had he worked?
   c. Did he tell the guard that he recognized Miles?
   d. Did he really recognize Miles?

4. **a.** Who wanted to see Hugh and Edith married before he died?
   b. What made Edith think that Miles would never return to Hendon Hall?
   c. How did Hugh treat Edith after they were married?
   d. Who had really written the letter?
5. **a.** When the prisoners went outside, what was Miles put into?
   b. Why was Miles put there?
   c. What did the guard threaten to do to Edward?
   d. Which character rode up at the end of the chapter?

PART E   Review Items

6. Use the words in the box to fill in the blanks.

flogged	betray
slumber	prosper
bind	armed
vagrant	reel
innocent	irritable
duties	penalty

a. When you are grouchy, you are
_____ .

b. Someone who is not guilty of doing
something wrong is _____ .

c. When somebody is beaten with a
whip or a switch, that person is
_____ .

d. Somebody who has a weapon is
_____ .

e. The things that you should do are
your _____ .

f. When you pretend to be somebody's
friend and then trick that person,
you _____ that person.

g. Another word for **stagger** is
_____ .

h. If you tie somebody up, you
_____ that person.

i. Another word for **sleep** is
_____ .

j. The punishment somebody receives
for breaking the rules is the
_____ .

PART F   Writing Assignment

Do you think that Edward's letter
would have convinced Hertford that
Edward was really the king?

Write at least **five** sentences that
explain your answer.

Lesson 117

PART A   Word Lists

1	2	3	4
ceremony	imagination	deafen	**New vocabulary**
procession	coronation	broken	1. riot
riot	concentration	brokenhearted	2. procession
imposter	expression	deafening	3. ceremony
aisle	hesitation	cannon	
	procession		

PART B   New Vocabulary

1. **riot**—A **riot** is a great fight that involves
a mob of people.
● What do we call a great fight that
involves a mob of people?

2. **procession**—A **procession** is a group of
people who go from one place to
another.
A line of people going through the
lunchroom is a **procession** of people
going through the lunchroom.
● A line of people going on a fire drill is a
_____ .

3. **ceremony**—A **ceremony** is an
important event that always takes place
in the same way.
A marriage is a **ceremony**. A
graduation is a **ceremony**.

PART C   Vocabulary Review

gossip	penalty
reel	armed
stocks	prison cell
deathbeds	deny
coronation	stall
smuggle	daily

1. **a.** When you hide something and take it to some place, you _____ something.
   b. If somebody hides some money and takes it into a prison cell, the person _____.

2. **a.** Another word for **everyday** is _____.
   b. What's another way of saying **She visited her grandmother everyday?** _____.
   c. What's another way of saying **He ate everyday?** _____.

3. People who are dying are on their _____.

4. A small room that prisoners live in is a _____.

5. An important event in which the crown is officially placed on the head of a new king is a _____.

6. **a.** When you say that something is not true, you _____ that thing.
   b. When you say you do not know a fact, you _____.
   c. When you say that you do not know a person, you _____.

7. **a.** When you tell rumors about something, you _____ about that thing.
   b. When you tell rumors about something you don't like, you _____.
   c. When you tell rumors about a new person in school, you _____.

8. When you try to put off doing something, you _____.

PART D   Story Items

1. **a.** At the beginning of Chapter 20, where was Edward?
   b. Who was holding Edward?
   c. Which character was smiling from his horse?
   d. Which character was in the stocks?
   e. Which character offered to take somebody else's punishment?
   f. Why do you think that character did that?
   g. What title did Edward give Miles?
   h. What other title did Miles already have?
   i. Miles almost cried because he had two strong feelings. One was humor. The other feeling was _____.

2. **a.** After Miles and Edward were free, which person did Miles decide to go see?
   b. Which city did Edward and Miles head for?
   c. At what time of night did they get there?
   d. What event was the mob of people celebrating?
   e. When was that event going to occur?
   f. Where did the riot take place?
   g. Who got separated?

3. **a.** How often did Tom Canty think about the real king?
   b. Tom hated himself when he thought about some people. Name those people.

4. **a.** What important event did Tom go to?
   b. What noises came from the Tower of London?
   c. The procession went from the Tower of London to _____.
   d. Which character rode next to Tom in the street?

5. Tom recognized someone in the crowd.
   a. Which character was that?
   b. What did that character do when Tom waved?
   c. What did Tom say to her?
   d. But how did Tom feel inside when he said that?
   e. What did Tom say to Hertford?
   f. What did Hertford think had happened to Tom?

PART E — Review Items

3. Use the words in the box to fill in the blanks.

identify	duties	prison cell
penalty	innocent	coronation
daily	deathbeds	smuggle
bound	stall	stocks
slumber	tragic	flogged
gossip	deny	

a. People who are dying are on their
_____.

b. When you hide something and you take it to some place, you
_____ something.

c. Another word for **sleep** is
_____.

d. When you say that something is not true, you _____ that thing.

e. When you tell what something is, you _____ that thing.

f. A device that was used to punish prisoners was called the
_____.

g. The things that you should do are your _____.

h. An important event in which the crown is officially placed on the head of a new king is a _____.

i. The punishment somebody receives for breaking the rules is the
_____.

j. When you try to put off doing something, you _____.

k. When you tell rumors about something, you _____ about that thing.

l. Something that is very sad is
_____.

m. Another word for **everyday** is
_____.

n. A small room that prisoners live in is a _____.

PART F — Writing Assignment

Do you think that Tom still likes being king?

Write at least **five** sentences that explain your answer.

Lesson 118

PART A — Word Lists

1	2	3
worthless	form	**New vocabulary**
heartless	platform	1. under arrest
hopeless	loud	2. imposter
motionless	aloud	
speechless	suspicious	
	suspicion	

PART B — New Vocabulary

1. **under arrest**—When a police officer places somebody **under arrest,** the officer accuses that person of committing a crime.

2. **imposter**—Someone who pretends to be somebody else is an **imposter.**
   - What do we call someone who pretends to be somebody else?

PART C   Vocabulary Review

deny
ceremony
stall
daily
procession
riot

1. **a.** A group of people who go from one place to another is a _____.
   b. A line of people going on a fire drill is a _____.
   c. A line of people going through the lunchroom is a _____.
2. An important event that always takes place in the same way is a _____.
3. A great fight that involves a mob of people is a _____.

PART D   Story Items

1. **a.** The ceremony was supposed to take place in a large _____.
   b. What kinds of people went into the church?
   c. What musical instruments announced the king?
   d. Why did Tom feel ashamed when he sat on the throne?
   e. What would happen to Tom once the crown was on his head?
2. **a.** Who interrupted the ceremony?
   b. Who did that person claim to be?
   c. Who agreed with that person's claim?
   d. Why was Hertford so surprised when he looked carefully at the two boys?
   e. Why did Hertford begin to ask Edward some questions?
3. **a.** How well did Edward answer the questions?
   b. Edward's descriptions did not satisfy Hertford because _____ could also give the descriptions.
   c. What object did Hertford ask Edward about?
   d. Hertford thought that the only person who could know where to find that object was _____.
   e. So, what would that person's answer prove?
   f. Edward said that the object was inside a _____.
   g. Who was ordered to go to the palace to look for that object?
4. **a.** As the crowd waited for news from the palace, they formed a ring around _____.
   b. Which person was left alone?
   c. What news did Lord Saint John bring?
   d. Now which person was left alone?
   e. What did Hertford threaten to do to Edward?
   f. Why wasn't Hertford able to carry out his threat?
   g. What did Tom ask Hertford to describe?

PART E   Review Items

5. Use the words in the box to fill in the blanks.

coronation	gossip
impulse	ceremonies
deathbeds	riot
deny	smuggle
stall	procession
intend	

a. An important event in which the crown is officially placed on the head of a new king is a _____.

b. A sudden, strong desire to do something is an _____.

c. When you hide something and take it to some place, you _____ something.

d. When you say that something is not true, you _____ that thing.

e. A group of people who go from one place to another is a _____.

f. If you plan to do something, you _____ to do that thing.

g. A great fight that involves a mob of people is a _____.

h. When you try to put off doing something, you _____.

i. When you tell rumors about something, you _____ about that thing.

j. Important events that always take place in the same way are _____.

PART F   Writing Assignment

Pretend that you are Tom Canty. Would you have said that Edward was the true king?

Write at least **five** sentences that explain your answer.

Lesson 119

PART A   Word Lists

1	2
incredible	product
impossible	produce
terrible	giant
horrible	garage
	garbage

PART B   Vocabulary Review

riot
ceremony
under arrest
procession
imposter

1. Someone who pretends to be somebody else is an _____.

2. When a police officer accuses a person of committing a crime, the officer places that person _____.

PART C   Story Items

1. a. Tom asked Hertford some questions about _____ .
   b. Did Tom know where that object was?
2. a. What would happen to Edward if Edward did not remember where he put the seal?
   b. Did Edward remember at first?
   c. Where did Edward say the seal was?
   d. Who was sent to find the seal?
   e. Lord Saint John was carrying _____ when he returned to the church.
   f. What did that object prove?
   g. What was the object supposed to be used for?
   h. What had Tom used the object for?
3. a. Who had Miles searched for all night long?
   b. Where had Miles stopped the next day?
   c. When Miles awoke, he decided to go to _____ .
   d. What did Miles hope to get from a lord?
   e. Who did Miles meet at the palace gate?
   f. What happened to Miles at the end of the chapter?

PART D   Review Items

4. Write what each character wanted from Oz.
   a. Scarecrow   c. Tin Woodman
   b. Dorothy   d. Lion

5. Write which breed of dog each statement describes. Choose from **airedale, collie, greyhound, hound,** or **poodle.**
   a. This breed is very fast.
   b. This breed is good at herding.
   c. This breed has a very sensitive nose.
   d. This breed may be the smartest.
   e. This breed is very brave.

6. **Use the words in the box to fill in the blanks.**

betray	procession	overcast
riot	imposter	flogged
ceremony	innocent	gagged
under arrest		

   a. Someone who is not guilty of doing something wrong is _____ .
   b. When you pretend to be somebody's friend and then trick that person, you _____ that person.
   c. When a police officer accuses a person of committing a crime, the officer places that person _____ .
   d. A great fight that involves a mob of people is a _____ .
   e. A group of people who go from one place to another is a _____ .
   f. Someone who pretends to be somebody else is an _____ .
   g. An important event that always takes place in the same way is a _____ .

PART E   Writing Assignment

Write at least **six** sentences that describe what Tom learned from his experiences as a king.

Lesson 120

PART A   Word Lists

1	2
delicious	gaze
suspicious	glaze
prosperous	desolate
dangerous	poverty
	ridicule
	ridiculous

PART B Story Items

1. Miles entered the throne room.
   a. Who was sitting on the throne?
   b. What did Miles do to see whether he was dreaming?
   c. What did the guards do?
   d. Who stopped the guards?
   e. Why was Miles about to sit in the presence of the king?
2. a. What titles had Edward given to Miles?
   b. Miles had tried to impress Edward days before by showing him _____.
   c. Which man did Miles see at the back of the throne room?
   d. What did Edward order the guards to strip that man of?
3. Tom Canty entered the room.
   a. Why was Edward pleased with Tom's rule?
   b. What would Tom have that nobody else could have?
   c. Where would Tom live?
   d. Who would live there with Tom?
4. a. Which country did Hugh move to?
   b. Who was never heard from again?
   c. Name at least **two** people that Edward rewarded.
5. a. While he was king, Edward changed the strict _____.
   b. When a lord challenged Edward, Edward would say, "What do you know about _____?"
      • churches • suffering • lords
   c. How old was Edward when he died?
   d. How was he different from the other kings in Europe at that time?

PART C Review Items

6. **Use the words in the box to fill in the blanks.**

take advantage	prosper	vagrant
merciful	innocent	identify
regret	stocks	impulse
riot	convince	tragic
betray	irritable	capable of
retreat	intend	

a. When you are grouchy, you are _____.
b. When you are sorry about something that happened, you _____ that thing.
c. If you plan to do something, you _____ to do that thing.
d. The opposite of **cruel** is _____.
e. Something that is very sad is _____.
f. When a person is helpless and you make that person do what you want, you _____ of that person.
g. A sudden, strong desire to do something is an _____.
h. When you move backwards, you _____.
i. When you pretend to be somebody's friend and then trick that person, you _____ that person.
j. A person who does not have any place to live and has no job is a _____.
k. Someone who is not guilty of doing something wrong is _____.
l. When you earn money and do well, you _____.
m. When you make somebody believe something, you _____ that person it is true.
n. When you tell what something is, you _____ that thing.

PART D Writing Assignment

Edward is no longer a pauper.

Write at least **six** sentences that describe what Edward learned from his experiences.